A Step-by-Step Guide to

Intuitive Wellness™

Create Wellness
In Your Body, Mind and Soul
by Utilizing Your Intuitive Power

A Step-by-Step Guide to

Intuitive Wellness ™

*Create Wellness
In Your Body, Mind and Soul
by Utilizing Your Intuitive Power*

Laura Alden Kamm

*Intuitive Therapeutics Publications
A Division of Mayflower Press
Scottsdale, Arizona, USA*

Intuitive Therapeutics Publications
A Division of Mayflower Press
Scottsdale, AZ
U.S.A.

Copyright 1999 Laura Alden Kamm
founder@energymedicine.org

First Edition U.S.A. 1999

Printed in USA.

ISBN 0-9675608-0-2

Dedication

To my parents:
Mary Alden Kamm and Rev. Dr. Roland Travers Kamm

Your love, patience and wisdom have been ever present,
shimmering through your hearts and eyes
and into my life.

You exemplify all that I wish to become,
generous caregivers of human kind

I dedicate this work to you both
with unceasing gratitude and love,
for you have held me, nudged me forward
and stood beside me always

You are my angels here on earth.

Acknowledgments

Beyond my gratitude for all that I have and the omnipresent source from which it comes, my sincerest and heartfelt thanks must go to Dr. Albert Camma. It was he who, in 1981, skillfully escorted me back from death. Without you, Dr. Camma, and the assistance of your team, I would not have had the joys and challenges of being human for these years hence. I express to you my deepest sense of gratitude and cannot help but ponder the karma between us that allowed you to magically pop into my life at such a perilous, yet auspicious time.

I would also like to acknowledge my brother, John Alden Kamm, and my dear sisters, Christine Deitz and Katie Cursio. My love and support are always with you, as yours have been with me -- what a blessed family we are. To their loved ones, who are mine as well, thank you for all of your love and encouragement through the years.

To my two children Alicia and Christopher -- needless to say, the two of you will forever dance in my heart, as you are the most precious part of my life. To Barbara Kamm, who has blessed my life by her glee-filled and comforting heart. And to Linda Kamm, thank you for believing in me; it matters more than you know. To Geoffrey (Babu) Morris, I express my profound gratitude to you for your love, continuous support and caring. It is such a comfort to know that you are there for me.

So much gratitude I offer to Rose Winters, Diana Hunt, Candy Southwick, Lorie Geare, Ginnie Livingston and Irene Conlan. Thank you all for your visionary efforts, endless love and assistance in furthering my work. I bless the laughter and the absolute joy you bring to my life. I do so love you all and appreciate your presence and support in my life.

I would like to also acknowledge Dr. Gladys Taylor McGarey, the mother of holistic medicine, for her years of service and contributions to the field of medicine, as well as for her contribution to this work. What an honor to have had our paths cross! A heartfelt thanks goes, as well, to The Gladys Taylor McGarey International Medical Foundation for its support.

A special thanks to Chuck and Judy Theisen. You both have touched my life in so many ways, and have helped bring a dream to life. As well, my gratitude extends to Cathy Stuart. Cathy, there is no doubt that the angels brought us together. For through my dreams I was led immediately to you. We both took flight from there. My love and gratitude are with you always. And a special thanks goes to Sherry Butler. Thank you for your brilliant ideas which helped launch a very important time in my life. I would also like to acknowledge Joseph Christopher Kosko -- your soul loved mine so much that you came to be my greatest teacher. I truly honor and acknowledge your presence in my life and the many talents you possess.

Several people wove their energy through the editing process of this work and I thank all of you for your assistance.

My eyes could not have done this alone. Each of you, in your own way, took a tremendous burden off my shoulders and helped me literally see my way through this process. To Lindsey Hicks, whose wise watchful eyes played such an important role in the final editing of this book. The joyful, enthusiastic and precise manner of your work demonstrates, so beautifully, the way in which you move through the world and touch others. Thank you for gracing these pages with your heart, mind and artistic talents. I would also like to thank Anton Byers for his editing skills early on in this work. I am grateful to you for your perspective and words of wisdom. And to Karen Gray who graciously took my hand and led me around the last corner -- thank you, Karen.

To all my friends and loved ones who live across the country, I thank you all for putting up with my schedule, so I can do the work of my heart. I cherish you all deeply. From the Northwest to the Northeastern shores, all of you will dance in my heart always.

Most humbly, I wish to thank and acknowledge the people who have entrusted me with their energy in the context of my work. I honor all of you so very much, as you are the truest and bravest pioneers regarding the healing and evolution of the soul.

Contents

Foreword

By *Gladys Taylor McGarey, M.D.,M.D(H)*

I have been practicing medicine for over 50 years and have watched remarkable changes take place in the field of medicine, both in therapy and in diagnosis. When I was in medical school, we were still radiating the thymus gland when an X-ray of a child's chest picked up the fact that it was enlarged. We now know that the thymus gland is the master gland for the reticuloendothelial system and was enlarged because the child needed the enabling energies this gland produced. We would never think of destroying the thymus gland today. We also took tonsils out if they were enlarged just because they were there, not realizing that they, too, had an important part to play in healing

This I have seen repeated over and over again as we have learned more and more about the human body and the magnificent way in which it works. We know so much more now than we did then. However, we are just beginning to learn what the mind and emotions do in relationship to our physical body and have not even begun to touch how the spirit and soul relate to the body in which we live.

Ever since I began working with the Edgar Cayce material in 1955, I have become more aware of the reality regarding the statement which comes from these readings, "the spirit is the life, the mind is the builder, the physical is the result," and how this is an integral part of how we manifest and live in a third dimensional world. Our spirit is the energizing force, the light, the life. The mind is the connecting bridge between the spirit and the physical body, and it is the way in which we deal with our thoughts, our decisions, our will, our perceptions and ourselves that manifests in our physical body.

It's very exciting to me to watch my colleagues and my patients become more aware of the part they play in their own healing. These awarenesses demonstrate the effect that their choices, simple choices and great choices, have on their body's function(s) and how it responds to the world around it. We are becoming aware that illness is not punishment, but a way in which our soul can bring to our conscious mind the lessons that we need to learn and ways in which we can learn them. This is not condemnation by an angry God, but a loving experience through which we manifest our soul's expression. We're finding that there is an ever increasing number of books about the dimension of consciousness through which people move and the effect that this has on the physical body.

In this remarkable book, Laura Alden Kamm has shown us her own journey and given us ways in which we, too, can participate in this transformational process. I truly believe that we are in a time when all of us, if we so choose, can access the healing power that is in our bodies, our minds and our spirits.

Perhaps a new race is evolving with an added awareness which we have not known prior to this time, and as this race, we now evolve. This book will be helpful in guiding us as we learn ways in which to adjust and evolve as more spiritual beings.

Preface

Above is the Tibetan symbol for OM, the universal harmonic of God. Notice, if you will, that directly below the circle are two lines that resemble a bird's wings. Buddhism, as well as other great philosophies, espouse that in order for us to achieve enlightenment, or God- consciousness, we need to apply the wisdom we innately know and have learned from our life and teachers. This is what this book symbolizes. I suppose you could use this analogy to understand more clearly my intention for this work: avionics engineers who understand only the theoretical mechanics of flight are vital for a person who wishes to understand flight. Nonetheless, their experience is theory bound. If you wanted to learn how to fly, you would need to ask yourself if you wanted an engineer or a pilot to instruct you. In short, would you want someone who knew simply the theory or someone who knew both theory and its application?

Throughout my life's path I have been drawn into the body experience first, and then I stumble or fall over the literature to back up or validate my experience. That, perhaps, is the path of an empathic person. To learn it you've got to get it into the body first. This way of experiencing life gives greater depth of understanding to one's journey. Luckily, we are all empathic, to varying degrees, and therefore, this ideal applies to all of us. In order for us to learn something, really learn and embrace it, it has to be directed into the spirit, into the mind and then into the body.

As a child I knew that all paths lead to the same door, and that there are just different knocks. My spiritual childhood experiences demonstrated this to me very clearly. As I grew into an adult, my illness and near-death experience brought forth many bodily challenges and experiences. Obviously, not only my body was involved, my mind and spirit were challenged as well. After which, literature from ancient religions and philosophies brought me peace regarding these soulful experiences and encounters.

Look again at the symbol of OM. Look at the wings. Just as a bird or butterfly needs two wings to fly toward its destination, we too need two wings as we fly through our lives toward enlightenment. One wing, the left wing, is your innate wisdom and the wisdom you gain from knowledge and understanding the world in and around you as you experience it. The left wing is your feminine nature, the divine mother, who carries the consciousness of intuition. Your intuition, and the further development of it, will bring you greater knowledge of self and deeper levels of understanding, from which your wisdom will develop and grow. The other wing, the right wing, is the masculine, the divine father, which is the consciousness through which action is applied. It is the wing of method.

My prayer is that this book will provide for you a sampling of both wisdom and method, both of which simply need to be awakened and recognized as being within you already. As you read and work with that which resonates within you, and within the context of this book, I am confident that your own wings of wisdom and method will come forth, assisting you in flying home to your source with greater harmony and peace.

1

My Path to Becoming a Medical Intuitive

I wasn't always a medical intuitive — someone who has the skill to locate and discern disorders and diseases within the human body using intuitive and energetic means. Moreover, I will always look upon my initiation into becoming a medical intuitive as a gift. I feel that way now, but at the time, this "gift" came wrapped around mind-searing pain and a life-threatening illness. So, I often refer to this illness and the experiences within it as the most "wonderfully awful thing" that has ever happened to me.

It was Superbowl Sunday, January 1982, and I awoke with a severe headache and vomiting. The following morning, I felt even worse and knew I needed to get medical help. The doctor told me that I had the flu and a sinus infection and promptly sent me home with some medications and the typical instructions — drink plenty of fluids and rest. At that time, my children were three and four years old. My husband was working out of town, so there was no time for rest. As far as the medications and fluids were concerned, any attempt to put or keep them in my body was to no avail. My body rejected everything — nothing stayed down. Three more days passed and my symptoms worsened. I felt as if my life was moving in slow motion. By Thursday morning I had lost 17 pounds due to the relentless retching.

On a level that lies somewhere beyond the physical, something else was happening inside of me. There was an obscure, small voice rattling around in my head. This voice was telling me that I needed to get back to the doctor. It was telling me that I didn't have the flu and that something was terribly wrong. Somehow, I understood that this inner whisper was speaking the truth.

As a result of my illness, I began to unveil a hidden wisdom within me — a source that had lapsed from my consciousness. After all, I had been too busy *doing* life, and living out my role as a mother, wife and college student. I had lost touch with my deeper self — especially when the demands of life moved me away from my fundamental being, my core, my God/Goddess within.

I had misplaced my internal doctrines of truth and wisdom having pushed them so far off that I had even forgotten the conceptual lifelines that tethered me to them. The consequence of this was that the deepest and truest aspects of myself had been lying dormant for years, covered by the debris of external authority and the sticky energy of appeasement and compliance. Thank God these lifelines were still there and were being unearthed by my soul as it cried out through the expression of this illness. I had begun to pay attention.

On that same Thursday morning, I drove myself back to the doctor. My regular physician was not available, so another doctor within the same medical group saw me. This doctor reaffirmed my physician's earlier diagnosis of flu and a sinus infection and sent me home with even stronger medications.

When I arrived home from the doctor's office, it was without hesitation that I called my mother and father in Ohio and told them what was happening. I remember how odd it was that I even called. After all, I had certainly had the flu before and had managed to take care of my children and my life without their assistance. I didn't quite understand what made the voice inside of me speak out, prompting me to call. Through my growing awareness of this inner voice, I was developing a strong sense that there was something really ominous about this illness. My mother must have sensed it too, because she insisted that I come to Ohio so that she could take care of the children and me.

When I arrived, it felt good to be in my parents' home and in their loving care, but a weekend passed and I was no better. I decided to see a local physician, a family friend. He was most sympathetic but didn't know what was wrong with me either. Because I had lost so much body fluid from the continuous vomiting, I decided to check myself into the hospital later that day. It was obvious to me that I had crossed a threshold and needed professional care. During the check-in procedures at the hospital, they ran some tests to see if they could pin down the cause of this illness. The tests concluded that I was pregnant, which was definitely a false reading according to what I knew of my body. Nonetheless, the hospital and the doctors didn't listen to me. The test results stood strong — I was pregnant, with the flu and a sinus infection.

Days passed and the pain in my head became unbearable. My eyes started to protrude from their sockets. My frustrated doctors frantically ordered test after test: abdominal and uterine ultrasounds, upper and lower GI's, and continual blood work. So far, there were no answers. I could feel that the energy of life that supported and filled my body was drying up. I knew I was dying.

The days melted away, liquefied by the hospital monotony. I was not amused by my situation or by the mechanics behind the caring. Regularly, a nurse would enter my room, smile, and replace the IV drip bag, which had become a part of me — new liquids for the body, new oil for the machine. Some nurses had the audacity to say "Now honey, are you sure you aren't pregnant?" I continued to lie in my bed — afraid, weak and incensed.

The physical pain was now competing with my inner voice for my mind's attention and focus. I knew there was something important about the presence of this inner voice and its connection to my illness. I was frustrated as it offered no precise definition of what was happening to me, although I knew it murmured some form of internal distress signal from my soul.

I felt fear like I never had before. I would squirm around in my hospital bed, moving my legs up and down, readjusting my body in hopes that it would fine-tune my inner voice's words and allow me to understand them more clearly. Uneasiness expanded within me, along with the pain in my head, which had become thunderous and out of control. On Saturday, my thoughts began to spiral in tornado-like confusion. I wanted answers to calm my fears. I wanted something to ease the shattering pain in my head, which had increased, spawning a cruel inner racket that I feared could only be silenced by death. My apprehension escalated. I was afraid of falling asleep — afraid of its darkness and potential eternity. I wondered — if I dared close my eyes would I again see the sun weave its mantle of colors through an early morning sky?

I remember lying on a gurney waiting to be taken into X-ray for another test and looking despairingly into my mother's face. As I threaded my fingers through her soft hands, I pleaded with her, "Get me out of here. This is killing me. I'm dying." Her eyes dropped, scanning my body and her grip increased affectionately and helplessly. Her soft, unwrinkled face was twisted with concern — she knew. Many years later my mother painfully told me that I had looked like a broken old man — the person she knew as her Laura was gone.

5

I didn't want to leave my family, my two beautiful children Alicia and Christopher, my husband, parents, brother and sisters, my friends, and my gardens — I didn't want to leave anyone or anything. My children were so young. I wanted to watch them grow up. I wanted them to remember their mother and how much she loved them. I wanted to share with them the things I had been taught and shown as a child, which had meant so much to me. I was afraid that I would only be remembered through some corner-worn photographs scarcely capable of conjuring up any interpretation of my face, my actions and my love for them. My heart reached out to hold on to my children and family, clinging to them.

Tears of silent terror streamed down my face as these notions tore through my heart and mind. I wasn't certain if I could reach beyond the dark gates that this illness had set before me and get well again. I felt trapped in a body that was being devoured by a nameless disease. I lay there alone, out of control, my body soaked with panic. Powerless, I felt that there was nothing I could do.

My eyes continued to become extremely sensitive to light since the onset of this illness and the doctors didn't know why. Due to this heightened light sensitivity, the venetian blinds, which hung vertically in the window of my room, remained closed. During the day, slivers of light would steal though the cracks in the blinds. As the hours passed, I noticed how the light crept along the wall. It was my only indication of the hours passing — a measuring stick of sorts. Even the small emergency light that remained on above the doorway played havoc with my eyes. Any light demanded more strength than my eyes or willpower were able to generate. Darkness remained the shade of my room, and of my mood.

Waves of horror swept across my face as I looked at myself in the bathroom mirror. I would question, *Who belongs to this face? Who is attached to this ghoulish shell?* My skin had taken on a foreign texture and color — a sallow greenish-gray — and my eyes continued to bulge from their sockets. In just a few short days, I was disappearing, being replaced by something that was beyond sickly. Where was I going, and why?

As the sun rose on the eleventh day, I was lying in my hospital bed surrounded by my loving family and concerned doctors. We all sensed the impending, however, not knowing why I was dying magnified the collective frustration. Although those around me were bewildered, something inside of me was changing. My internal voice was giving me direction, even if it was to seemingly minor degrees. It was burgeoning forth with fresh awareness and I sensed a new journey unfolding, presenting itself in calm silence. No longer did I share the concerns of those who were gathered around me.

My awareness of this reality, an imprisoned reality that I had constructed within the shallow limits of my five senses, was beginning to fade. My spirit was beginning preparations for its transcendence. Muted thoughts of peace began to gently weave throughout my body, and I knew these sensations of tranquillity were indications of what was to come. These new perceptions flooded my mind, giving me a directional push toward the realization that everything that was happening was filled with an exalted purpose, orchestrated by some universal force which I could only sense at the time. I looked around at my family and the doctors as they discussed yet another series of tests. They were trying so hard to figure out what was killing me. Pulling my thoughts back inside of myself, I waited.

Later that afternoon, my family chose to leave my hospital room so that I could rest. I was alone — alone with this fresh awareness. I was a bit perplexed that, rather suddenly, the chronic sensations of foreboding that had plagued me for days were gone. The pain, which had become such a part of me, had shifted, transmuting itself so gently, yet so profoundly, that the realization of its absence was genuinely shocking. A powerful feeling began accelerating throughout my body, chilling me. My mind and body were passing through a gateway into a different dimension, traveling to a new level of consciousness.

"Could this really be happening?" The words resonated deep within me. Wonderment and curiosity enveloped me, as my mind searched for answers. Fully cognizant, I was able to discern my thoughts, reality, physical condition and surroundings; yet, I was profoundly aware that my soul had begun its process of separation from my physical body. I was in a state of absolute awe.

I could feel my soul like never before and, without warning or provocation, I began to see, with my physical eyes, what I could only describe as my soul lifting up and moving away from my body. Watching intently, I saw and felt the vigor of my soul lighten further as it floated upward, forming itself into this beautiful, pale, bluish-white fog, hovering 4-6 inches above me. Then, the part of my body from which the energy or soul had left turned to a heavy, sodden-like gray.

Quaking and shuddering, I watched as this occurrence repeated itself. It began, at first, with sections of my legs and arms, finally, moving upward through the trunk of my body. I was inundated with a thick and heavy feeling. I felt as if my soul's light was becoming less and less present within me. Nonetheless, I still felt connected. I knew I was alive and aware of what was happening. Assurance swept over me, whispering into my heart, telling me that I was watching my soul perform a primordial dance that it had done a thousand times before.

It was as if I could sense some system that consisted of multidimensional layers of my body — the scientific bent to my personality could not help but engage as I continued to focus on what was transpiring. I attempted to identify the particulars within each layer; however, they were extremely subtle and, therefore, only slightly perceivable. Discernment was difficult, even within my own mind — I had absolutely no framework or reference point for this type of occurrence. Even with these difficulties, my curiosity pressed forward, continuing to look at and feel into those magical layers, which seemed to be four or five in number.

I sensed that my soul was separating, pulling away in a taffy-like manner and freeing itself from its bodily constraints. It felt as if my body's energy was intertwining with something distant and unnamed. I began to feel light and airy in comparison to my physical body, which felt dull and weighted down with disease. The light of my soul was also changing; I could feel its effervescent energy leaving. Ironically, as this bubbling essence lifted away, my heart felt lighter. I felt stronger, or perhaps it was my consciousness that felt stronger as my body continued to drift into a seemingly detached, weighty place of nonexistence.

Before this illness I was more or less unaware of the river of energy that flowed inside of me. However, at this moment, this life force was drying up and beginning its unconstrained journey home. Slowly and purposefully, I was being reintroduced to a sense of archetypal freedom — an ancient, innate wisdom trickled through my consciousness.

Freedom and serenity swept through me. I knew who I was; I knew where I came from and I knew what my purpose for being was. More importantly, I was not afraid anymore. This sense of remembering and the connection I had with God and Spirit brought a heartfelt understanding of the meaning behind everything that was happening. Along with this awareness came its companion — peace.

It was like someone had turned on a movie inside my head, mind's eye, or inner vision, which had become extraordinarily lucid. I was seeing in a strange and seemingly magical way. I could see the spaces between the walls of my physical body. I could see the bones, the muscles and the blood. I could see with my eyes closed or opened. As I continued to observe my soul separating itself from my physicality, this inner vision took me into different levels and, occasionally, I felt as if I had some directional control over what was happening. As I looked at the outside of my body, I watched the energy moving in and around me. I then turned my attention back inside my body and was able to see into the bones and tissues of my legs and study the myriad of colorful energies as they danced throughout. I was able to visually telescope down into the measureless spaces of emptiness and could see my soul leaving what looked to be the molecules and atoms that construct my body. I was able, by some mysterious force, to witness deep within these infinitesimal parts of my body, observing the miraculous separation of spirit and matter.

I was totally absorbed. I felt as if nothing were beyond this new inner vision of mine. Although I didn't fully understand what was happening, I did realize several things. I knew my role was to be an observer, to let things happen and to pay attention. It was further apparent that I didn't have much control over this vision. Still, I had no real clue as to the origin of this projector-like way of seeing. Everything was transpiring so quickly.

I had a sense that part of me was awakening and moving onward. Everything illustrated the magnitude and limitlessness of life. It was with that recognition and acknowledgment that I knew I was limitless as well. I was dazzled with wonderment, yet, reverent humility enveloped me. I knew that if I somehow survived and managed to become well again, I *would* remember everything about this phenomenally holy experience. Certainly, I was witnessing the relinquishing of the interwoven connections between physical matter (my body) and my soul. My countenance was immersed in the inclusive acceptance of this gentle process — my own physical death.

My thoughts shifted away from my previous fears concerning leaving my family and friends to readiness. I wanted to leave this body. Again, I was not afraid. My body felt doltish and cumbersome and I became aware that this vehicle, my body, was no longer necessary to the gateway I was about to pass through. I was caressed by a loving calm so graceful and sweet that I hungered for more. No longer did I struggle or attempt to coerce my body back to wellness. Fear, which had been hovering over me like a vulture, soared away.

As I let go of my former attachments to my family and to the life that I knew, enormous amounts of relief welled up in my being, engulfing me like torrential flood waters overflowing their once restrictive gates. I was drenched with a quieting serenity — nothing earthly mattered. I knew this journey — my journey — was simply moving into another dimension. I knew it was a place to which my spirit would return. I would soon become, once again, a more aware and divine being of energy. I was going to a place where God and I would become one.

For those friends and family members who remained, I knew I would never be forgotten by them because of our spiritual connection. I would be linked to them through thoughts, feelings and through their memories of me. I knew we would see each other again. Information flooded my mind and heart, reminding me that we all return to the *one* source.

It was much easier to be involved in the process because the excruciating pain no longer consumed my body. I was also mindful of the fact that I was not on any medication that could have caused me to imagine what was happening. Furthermore, I knew the seriousness of my physical condition. Although I didn't have control over the process of my dying, I could control my attitude. It was marvelous to watch the ultimate ritual of life and death as it unfolded within me. Curiosity continued to pursue me. *Is this what it feels like to die? How long does it take? Where did the pain go?* All of those questions dissolved into a place somewhere beyond thought. Gently embraced by the serenity of what I call God, I silently witnessed the process of death.

Thoughts raced joyously through my mind, bellowing inwardly in silence. My childlike spirit was vaulting inside, dancing and waiting for freedom to come. My body was indifferent, continuing to become even more weighted, apathetic and languid. Nevertheless, that encompassing bliss continued, dominating me and taking precedence over any prior existential concerns regarding my earthly existence. What was transpiring in and around me was a beautiful feat of nature. We often think of birth as creation and death as the end of creation. This glorious peace I was experiencing, on the multi-sensory levels of my being, was by no means an end — it was creation ablaze. A lightness and interconnectedness with all souls filled me. There was no time, no space. I was dying and at the same time being set free.

A whirling sound drifted slowly into my ears and head, rising and falling melodiously. The tone encircled me, carrying with it a peculiar familiarity that felt comforting. A continual parade of thoughts streamed through my mind, reassuring me that it was no longer necessary to suffer. Yet, I could not help but question the origin of those thoughts. Were they mine, or had someone or something whispered in my ear? My fears were transforming, allowing me to submerge into slumber.

The afternoon's experience fused with my sleep, and evening arrived along with some visitors. As they sat on the edge of the bed talking, their words passed over me. I was probing deep within, trying to rediscover the nuances of the encounter that had taken place earlier that afternoon. With my eyes closed, I sought reassurance. *Had I been dreaming?* I knew I had not been asleep when I watched the light lift away from my body. *Was this incredible inner vision real?* I didn't know what to make of that aspect of the situation. My logical, rational mind tried to discount what had happened. This experience and the sensations it brought with it were spiritual precepts. I finally concluded that there was no reason for me to deny my feelings. My heart's wisdom proclaimed the truth. This was a sacred rite of passage.

I didn't at that time ignore logic or rational thought. I used them in an attempt to determine the meaning behind this particular event. *What was behind the telescoping vision, the peace, and the knowledge? Was I going home to my spirit's dwelling place?* Any analyzing I did regarding the afternoon's encounter became cyclical within my mind, leading me back to my heart's answer — science and its truths lie in the mind; truth of self and my truth regarding this experience lie in the heart. I could longer deny the ringing in my heart, no matter what my mind was telling me. The truth was that my soul's exodus had begun that afternoon.

The pain returned that evening, reminding me of its unrelenting fervor, and offered a clearer identification by which I could gauge that afternoon's experience. Being pain free that afternoon and then having it return that evening was a valid indicator and comparison. And, the pain was most definitely back — boomeranging heavily within my body.

Now, the whirling sound and the curious thoughts dissolved into nothingness as the pain swelled to the forefront. I wrenched over on my side, sobbing. My family's voices broke through the solitude of my tears as everyone did their best to soothe me by speaking of happy family outings. My tears slowed as our thoughts joined together, remembering. Their love and caring was beautiful, unconditional and overwhelming. They were by my side, undaunted. Nonetheless, my family's love and desires for my wellness could not, at this time, bring about the cessation of this illness. There was a greater force at the helm, guiding me. I felt my life fading way.

I don't have any conscious memory of anything else pertaining to my physical body or my illness that evening. I wasn't told of the physical events that took place until several days later — and in some instances it was years before I knew everything that had happened to me. It took several years and, at times, a lot of courage to read through and feel the memories the medical documents conjured up.

The hospital had scheduled a CAT scan of my head with the hope of finally tracking down the origin of this illness. It was too late. *I was told much later that the pre-dawn shift of nurses came racing into my room after I had screamed out for help. I was told that I had gotten out of bed and gone into the bathroom but I had come out from the bathroom screaming, "I can't see! I'm blind!"* My eyes were protruding from their sockets in proportions that the nurses had never seen before. The doctors were quickly summoned and my family was called. They recommended an immediate transfer by ambulance to another hospital, 25 miles away. According to my physicians, it was my only hope.

I do not remember yelling for the nurse or telling them that I was blind. I do not remember being wrapped up and put on the gurney. Nor do I remember being loaded into the ambulance. I do remember floating inside a womb of gentle darkness — a place of peace, warmth and love. I had periodically felt that blissful sensation the day before. Now, it encompassed the totality of my being. I was surrounded by this warm, dark, gel-like substance that breathed life; yet, it held within it death. A void.

I felt no restrictions, no heaviness — only peace — and I embraced the tranquillity. Soothed by this place, my consciousness rested unaware of who I was or the life that I had just left. I was simply there, a being, an intelligence, floating in a place that was both full and empty, rising and falling within a primordial sea.

As if arising from a deep sleep, my consciousness began to shift, summoning forth an awakening. I then recognized a faint vibrating tone coming from somewhere around me. Initially, the vibrations from this sound were remote and indistinguishable, but the undulating tone grew more pronounced as the distance between us appeared to lessen. It raised no fear, only a sense of excitement and exhilaration, like that of an upcoming event. It was the same whirling sound I had heard before. I remembered its soft and velvet-like feel. It struck a cord deep within the center of my being, as my consciousness awakened further.

Instantly, the darkness was gone. I had broken free from this restful state, clear, vibrant and full of energy. At first, I didn't recognize that I had no physical body, as it lay in the ambulance, forgotten. My soul and my consciousness were aware that I — it — was up in the corner of the ambulance looking down at a pale, grayish woman. She lay there cold and undisturbed, oblivious to the tubes, wires and other medical equipment attached to her. I seemed to understand that she must have endured a tremendous ordeal in order to arrive at her present condition and appearance.

I remember observing the nurse lean forward, as if listening for her breath and whispering firmly in her ear, "Laura, hang on. Don't go yet. Come on, Laura, hang in there with me. It's not time for you to go." I watched the nurse's actions suddenly gathered momentum. Her tone and tempo filled with trepidation. "Come on! Come on! Come on! Come back! Laura, can you hear me? Come on, Laura!"

As I heard her speaking to this woman and calling her name, I realized that my body was on that cart, frozen with death. Moreover, I was glad to be rid of that body, away from a body so obviously riddled with the scourge of disease. Looking down at my former self, I watched the nurse lean forward toward the front of the ambulance, urging the driver to hurry, that she was losing me — that she had lost me. My husband later told me that while he was following the ambulance he was traveling over 100 mph, when suddenly the ambulance accelerated, speeding away from him at an unmatchable speed. He followed frantically. Again, as I read through the medical records. The report didn't state that I was dead or for how long. It simply noted, "No vital signs..."

I was unrestrained. No longer was the immobility of my body and its unmanageable limbs a consideration. Joy was overflowing, filling me with sensations that I had never experienced before. Continuing to hover in the corner of the ambulance, I became aware that not even the ambulance's tangible barriers could hold my spirit. I was able to float through the physical walls and still maintain a clear view of what was happening. I could see the blood pressure cuff on my arm, and the nurse listening and praying for my vital signs to return. I noticed that my long brown hair, which had been neglected from illness, pitched over the pillow's edge; an oxygen mask over my face; my eyes sickened and grotesque, bulging from their distorted sockets; and the sallow, grizzled color of my skin. I knew that this abhorrent sight wasn't me. I was dead. I was free.

Total liberation swept over me, surging and filling me with the reassurance of my return to the domain of the spirit. At that point, I experienced an acceptance of my most recent past, which immediately caused an emotional disconnection with that ashen body lying there. In that startling moment of disconnection, liberation pulsated through me, freeing me even further from the mental images of my former physical constraints. I was returning to my true home. I knew that my earthly body and existence was only a tiny part of the whole truth. My truth, at that moment, was that I was surrounded by freedom and heading home to the place of my origin. I soared onward into a place commonly known as the "tunnel."

Within that tunnel, I found myself flying upward at unparalleled speeds, yet not the least bit dizzying to my senses. Like a hurling comet, I went through the earthly boundaries, elongated with speed. In this dark place, I recognized the whirling sound as the same one I had heard before I left my body in the ambulance. Having that sound wrap around me now felt penetrating and reassuring. I was not afraid to be in this place. I embraced it.

I had a new body, similar to the physical body I had on earth only more pleasant; it was lighter and better balanced. I was a buoyant body full of energy. Information filled my mind and heart and I realized that this body was the essence that had made up my human body on earth. This was the life force I had seen disengage itself from my physical body while in the hospital. I could hardly believe that I felt so good and so full of love, for myself and my surroundings. It was obvious that I was made of light, love and a powerful pulsating energy. I felt fabulous!

There was no time. Although the speed at which I was traveling was evident by my earthly definitions, I knew that time was truly nonexistent. I also knew that there were no spatial dimensions beyond those limitations — simply eternity.

Suddenly, flashes of light began to appear around me. At first, they resembled spheres, which radiated a luminous white light. Then colors began to emanate from them and they began to take on a human-like form. The only way to describe this is to say that they were beings of light. I knew that these were others, like me, flowing within the rhythm of their own life-to-life transition. Some traveled through the tunnel faster than I did. Others stopped as if in a contemplative state, examining what was happening to them or questioning what they should do next. At one point, I was surrounded by so many of them that there were too many to count. Amazed, I could not help but stare at those around me. They were beautiful sparks of light with many distinct colors emanating from them, vibrant and sparkling. Everyone appeared to glow — a white light that came from deep within and radiated outwardly. Words sometimes turn colorless when attempting to define what I experienced.

As I approached the end of the darkness, I was catapulted out of the tunnel by a magnitude of force so powerful that it propelled me into the light, my arms and legs flailing. I stretched my body outward, grabbing toward the nothingness in a feeble human attempt to keep from falling. I felt awkward and off balance. Yet, I began to realize that I had not completely let go of my humanness.

I think back to this magnificent experience, and to this particular point and realize how ridiculous it was for me to be flailing around, clutching for things with the fear that I was falling. There I was dead, my spirit now fully alive in its most beautiful and natural state. Yet, my consciousness was still embedded with human-constructed realities, attempting to control things the old way. I had not yet fully let go. I wasn't trusting, even when my own spirit was trying to direct me. Imagine, not trusting my own spirit. How interesting. How hysterical. How sad.

As I collided with the full force of this powerful light it felt as if it had taken my breath away, slapping it from me as if I had taken the summer's first plunge into a glacial lake. Of course, I had no breath, but it is the only way I can describe the sensations in a way that is understandable. Thankfully, this most recent surge of panic was gone and I drifted into the charmingly glorious, responsive and love-filled light. I gasped with wonderment and childlike exhilaration at my newfound freedom that electrified my spirit. I was totally surrounded by the Light of God (both masculine and feminine), love and *universal intelligence,* all of which I perceived to be one in the same. I knew the answers to my questions that had plagued me earlier — a lifetime of questions. Strangely enough, memories of this place came soaring back in resounding bursts of energy, regaining their proper place within the very fiber of my spiritual being. This *was* the place of my origin — I was home.

As I became more aware of my surroundings, I screamed with joy; yet, no sound escaped my lips. It merely echoed within my heart. Radiant warmth encircled me like a freshly dried blanket — warmed by the gentle glow of a thousand friendly stars. I was full of love and acceptance. This was a holy place — and I was on a most sacred journey.

Within this new dimension, I began to feel the presence of others around me. The sensations grew and if I had skin, I would have had goose bumps rippling up and down my body. The veil or mist had lifted, revealing my destination. Around me stood magnificent beings. They were distinctly different from the sparks of light I had earlier encountered within the tunnel. I sensed it had something to do with what I'll call a deeper level of spiritual maturity, for they seemed to be well aware of and familiar with their surroundings. I knew they had been waiting for me and their warmth embraced me. I felt like dancing to the music that was now mysteriously filling my heart.

Let me preface these next sensations by saying that nothing of what I was experiencing happened in a way with which I was familiar. Nothing happened as it does in our physical world. I did not come upon this light, upon these beings as if I had simply walked into a room crowded with other people. Everything was slower; yet, it took no time at all. Because of the absence of time and space, and still having the need to describe this experience within the human framework of time and space, one can only attempt to grasp the paradoxes that existed. Everything occurred as if it were in slow motion, yet at blinding speed. Awarenesses or shifts in consciousness came gradually, yet flooded my being with incredible velocity.

Communication was from heart-to-heart and smile-to-smile. We spoke no words. Nonetheless, I felt pure love, acceptance and a total lack of judgment. As their welcoming words rang in my heart, a sense of reassurance swept over me. I understood every word they were conveying. Their countenance was holding me — embracing me — guiding me back to a full state of awareness. It seemed as if their energies were gently orchestrating the process of my remembering who I was as well as who they were.

As I stood in the glory of these incredible souls, I looked down at my feet and the light emanating from them startled me. My feet were aglow. I had seen this phenomenon from the others who stood around me, however, I had been so busy trying to be attentive to everything that it simply had not occurred to me to look at myself. My eyes traveled up and down my body, observing my own presence more carefully. I was astonished — the same dazzling spectacle was true for me as well. I was made of light!

The reality of the situation suddenly sank in. The pure energy that appeared to breathe outwardly from them bathed and filled me with love and devotion. I knew that the vital essence of this light, which permeated my being, came from a source deep within the chasms of my soul. I realized that this light energy *was* my soul. It was the sum and substance of my true nature. I was charged with amazing currents of love, marbled with reverence and wonder. All of those who had gathered around me seemed to be pleased with my childlike innocence.

I stood with this first group for what seemed like a long time. Then, without a hint as to what was going to happen next, I was suddenly transported to another environment. This place was a beautiful midnight-blue, and I couldn't tell if I was vertical, horizontal or at an angle. Surrounding me, as before, was another group of beings. This group was very different from the other group. Their demeanor radiated wisdom and intelligence in such a powerful way that it still astounds me to think of them. I felt such reverence and humility to be among them and feel their essence.

We walked for a while together in silence and came upon a structure that looked like a temple. It was crystalline in nature and unadorned. As we walked up the steps and entered, I noticed that there were others in the temple, similar to the beings who had been escorting me. Next, I became aware of the volumes and volumes of huge books. Books were opened before me and on the pages were scenes from my life, being played out as if I was watching a movie.

I recall seeing a particular scene from my childhood when I was about five or six years old. On a beautiful spring day, my best friend and I were doing our usual investigating around the neighborhood. I thought it would be a great idea if we could find a baby robin's egg, hatch it and raise it ourselves. I always wanted to have a robin for a pet. It didn't take us long before we found a nest cradled on a neighbor's ladder, which hung horizontally on the side of the garage. Since I was the taller of the two, it was my job to reach into the tightly woven nest and grab an egg. In our search for adventure, we had forgotten about the mother robin. Suddenly she came darting at my hand and head, chirping frantically and flapping her wings. We ducked and dodged the parental squawks and somehow, I managed to hang onto the egg. Dashing away with the tiny cobalt shell in my hand we headed towards my friend's backyard. Once there, we positioned ourselves on the picnic table ready to birth and then nurse this baby robin as our own. Bit by bit we gently chipped and peeled away the protective layers of the shell.

As I watched this scene play out before me, I recall feeling the excitement that pounded in my heart as I glimpsed behind the membrane of the egg and spied the tiny bird. I was surprised that I felt the same excitement all over again, only more so. That excitement soon turned into dread, as this miniaturized bird didn't look anything like what we thought a robin should look like. It was feeble, featherless and soon it was dead. We sat there, regarding our deed in horror-filled silence.

Remorse welled up inside of me in the presence of these sages. I not only felt my pain and sorrow, but felt my friend's, as well. Beyond that, I felt and absorbed the mother robin's panic and sorrow as she searched for her unborn baby. The worst sensation was that of the baby robin. I could feel the energy that was once inside that small, helpless creature. I continued to stand there, mortified.

Turning my focus back to the scene, I watched as we gently lay the pieces of eggshell and the dead baby robin to rest in my friend's backyard. Once again, I felt an overwhelming sense of loss for all. I was devastated. The heaviness of this burden brought awareness concerning the interconnectedness of all things and it smoldered deep within.

I was in the company of these beings for what seemed like a very long time — perhaps lifetimes. We communicated through heart-to-heart and intuitive means. We discussed my life, energy, healing and other topics. And like before, within a nanosecond and without warning, I was transported to another environment.

Now, I found myself standing on the outskirts of a beautiful forest. This glorious landscape was similar to that of a Monet or Manet painting. This forest was also filled with beings walking around in a contemplative state. Even though I wanted to go and speak to them, I also knew this was a sacred place, one of contemplation; therefore, I chose to stand on the periphery, observing. Then, I noticed a sensation moving up from my feet, sweeping through my body. It was electrical and filled me with such profound feelings of love and gratitude. I looked down and the grass upon which I was standing was glowing in the most extraordinary way. It was as if the grass were sending its love-filled energy and gift of unconditional love up through my body. In return, my gratitude literally rushed to form a fountain at the top of my head, allowing my heartfelt feelings to cascade down to the grass, refueling it. Through this experience, the powerful interconnectedness we have with all things was illustrated to me again.

Without warning, from behind me came a gargantuan being. If I were to measure it in understandable terms, I would have to say that this being was 30-40 feet in height. I didn't feel the need to turn and see who was there. This male-like energy radiated such love and warmth that I felt overwhelmed. I felt childlike. Our communication assured me that I would be most welcome if I chose to stay in this place. I was also told that I had some things to do, some tasks to accomplish, and that it would be beneficial to my soul's growth and evolution to return and attend to these matters. At that moment, my children's faces and pictures of the rest of my family flashed in front of my mind's eye. My heart and soul had made a choice.

The next thing I remember was a voice saying, "Do you know where you are? Do you know your name? Do you know who the President is?" This wasn't a radiant being talking to me; it was a nurse in the neuro-ICU unit at the hospital. I had just awoken from a coma and discovered that through the initial diagnostic test when I had arrived at the hospital that I had abscesses in the right occipital lobe of the brain — a very rare condition. These abscesses were caused by an even rarer set of circumstances.

Prior to my becoming ill in late January of 1982, I had a cyst removed from the back of my head in my doctor's office in July of 1981. At that time the doctor pointed out that the cyst he had just removed had little brown hairs growing on it.

What made it unusual was that these hairs were growing inward, toward my brain. By removing the cyst a

27

chain of physiological events took place over the next seven months.

This cyst was part of a rare type — dermoid cyst. That means the cyst is connected to a benign tumor by a hollow tube. In my case, the cyst was located at the midline at the back of the skull; the hollow tube traveled down through my skull and was attached to the benign tumor located in the right occipital lobe. The dermoid cyst formed while I was in my mother's womb. It was the beginning of another child, my twin. Unfortunately, the twin didn't form past a certain cellular level and the cells that did form lodged in my head while I was continuing to develop and thus created the dermoid cyst phenomenon.

Finally, we knew the strange cause of this illness. The doctors also detected that I had a severe case of spinal meningitis. It was the spinal fluid that was causing my eyes to extend from their sockets. The increase in fluid tried to find some point of release. The doctors then pumped me full of the strongest antibiotics known to science with the hope of encapsulating the abscesses in an attempt to avoid surgery. Those attempts lasted about a week when I began to get that sinking feeling again. Tests revealed that surgery was needed, as the encapsulation attempts had not worked.

My doctor, Albert Camma, was another miracle that occurred in my life. Fortunately, I landed in his capable, saintly hands within this medium-sized town in Ohio. Dr. Camma

was then, and is today, a top neurosurgeon. He told me that I
would be home with my family in eight days after a two-hour
surgery. What I didn't know was that he told my family that it
would be a difficult operation and that if I did live through it, I
could end up possibly blind or a vegetable. He was doing his
job — keeping me in the most hopeful, calm state I could
possibly be in, while being completely honest with my family in
reference to the risks involved with this type of surgery.

The surgery surprised everyone. Instead of taking only
a few hours, it took seven and a half. The abscessed material
had somehow wound its way through the convolutions of my
brain and the surgery was much more intricate than previously
thought. I awoke that evening in neuro-ICU with my husband
by my side and a turban made of gauze wrapped around my
head.

The next morning the nurses were all chattering at me,
as they swung my bed over toward the window. They were
smiling and telling me that they had to show me something.
Outside my window, perched on a tree branch sat a squat little
robin. This was no ordinary robin — it had a white head. This
adorable albino-headed robin was attached to a cute little
red-breasted body. The nurses and everyone in my family
teased me, remarking that with his white head he looked just
like me. I knew, however, why the bird was there. He was my
messenger. He was, in my eyes and heart, sent from beyond to
say that everything was going to be all right. He sat there on
that the branch for the three days and nights that I was in ICU.
When I was moved to another room, a nurse told me that as

soon as I left, the bird flew away. He had completed his mission.

Within a few months, I had physically recovered from the ordeal, slowly getting my physical strength back. I felt fortunate because I had regained all but a portion of my physical sight — I was blind in the left visual field in both eyes. In spite of my joy at having survived, I was now experiencing some interesting visual challenges that went beyond learning to deal with the blindness. I struggled because I wasn't able to drive myself anywhere, which made me dependent on others to do the everyday errands. I also found myself bumping into things so often that I had bruises all over the left side of my body.

It was the occurrence of some odd visual experiences that really scared me, making me think that the demons that caused this illness in the first place were back. I began to think that my doctor had not removed all of the abscessed material. I was seeing bands and circles of colors around things. At first, I started to see them around birds and plants and shortly thereafter, I noticed them around people. I didn't want to tell anyone about these occurrences; after all, I had just had brain surgery, and telling people I was now seeing colors around things would have not been the right thing to do. I was convinced that everyone would think I was crazy — primarily because I thought I was crazy.

So, I went back to my doctor in Ohio and he assured me that I was fine. He told me, in a matter of fact manner, that I was seeing fields of energy. I believed him, but was hesitant.

The last time I saw this type of energy I was as a young girl of fifteen, and when I shared those experiences with people I was told by external authorities that what I had seen and felt didn't exist. I was now reacting to this situation from that rejected point of view of that young teenage girl. *How could energy exist now when I was told that it didn't exist then?*

In an attempt to push these visual anomalies out of my way and to prove to myself that I was healthy and normal, I decided to enroll at the university to test my mental abilities. I had to prove to myself that I wasn't crazy, and that having extensive brain surgery hadn't affected me. I took classes that would draw upon both left and right brain abilities. I needed to find out if, indeed, any of my cognitive pistons were misfiring. I took economics, nutritional chemistry, art and an applied design class along with a technology construction design class. I got a 4.0 average. After the semester was over and I sat down to think about what I had just accomplished and it finally sank in that I was OK.

After all, look at what I was able to do — take care of two children, a house, a husband who worked out of town and my schoolwork — and now partially blind as well. I was finally able to let go of the notion that I was ill and that what I was seeing was bad. I didn't know what to do with it as of yet; therefore, I decided to let it be and move on with my life.

As the months turned into years, I kept my near-death experience to myself. Occasionally, I would make elusive comments, leaving out any details. I simply didn't have a context for this experience, and therefore, I felt alone and unsupported. There was one bit of confirmation about my near-death experience that came from my sister and a friend in Indiana. Both told me, at separate instances, experiences they had at the exact same time that I was in the ambulance. I thought it interesting that neither my sister nor my friend knew one another and that they lived in two different states.

My sister told me that on the morning that I slipped away in the ambulance, she was getting ready for work when she saw me standing at her dresser in her bedroom. She said that it felt like I was trying to communicate with her, and that I was telling her good-bye. She knew I was sick and in the hospital, but she never knew that I was *that* sick, as my mother didn't tell her the grimness of my situation.

My friend in Indiana told me that I had come to her in a dream that morning, also saying goodbye. These two occurrences happened minutes apart and both encounters gave me a spark of validation that what I had experienced was true.

After my recovery, I continued on with my life doing the best that I could. My husband and I were having marital troubles. We had married at a young age and had come from very different lifestyles and belief systems. After two children, these differences were now making the situation uncomfortable, but I didn't want to break up the family.

At the time, I was fulfilled with my children and owning businesses. My husband, on the other hand, was not happy with his life or work. He was trying to find his happiness outside of himself and therefore wanted to move the family in an attempt to make *our* lives better.

The move to Washington was nothing short of divine guidance. In retrospect, I am grateful to my husband that we moved there. I absolutely loved living in Washington. We lived in a small town, nestled on an island in the Puget Sound north of Seattle. For me, it was like heaven on earth. I was completely connected to the nature of the setting. It was as if I had come home to live in a magical land in which my soul could expand and soar.

It was a totally charming place. In order to get to the island from the mainland, you had to take a ferry. It was on one of those many ferry rides that my work as a medical intuitive came forth.

Early one day, my husband had slammed a car trunk lid on his hand. As we stood on the bow of the ferry, he told me what happened and showed me his hand. I cupped my hands around his and simply held them. At that moment, my hands suddenly became hot. Then the telescoping inner vision, which I had not experienced since I had been ill, came back, and I was now looking at a hot red and yellow core that illustrated the pain he was experiencing deep within his hand. I could also hear and sense the screams of pain from each of the affected cells.

The color around his hand was very vivid. I was surprised by what I was seeing; however, this experience was the harbinger of my future. I remember standing very still and feeling the sea air blow through my hair. Going deep into the experience, I felt and sensed everything around me. It was as if I were watching, feeling and existing in another dimension far apart from the world where my body was standing. All of a sudden, everything clicked. A cosmic wheel had finally found the right notch, allowing it to turn unencumbered and without struggle. Now, I knew what was happening to my hands and my altered state of vision became normal for me. This offered stability and calmness to my entire being. After a few moments, I let go of his hands and the visions and sensations let go as well.

The next morning, the children and I had just finished breakfast when my husband came downstairs waving his hand, saying, "I don't know what you did to my hand yesterday on the ferry, but it doesn't hurt any more." I wasn't quite sure what I had done either, but I was ready to learn more.

We all have teachers in our lives. Life's experiences, the wonders of nature and other people who weave in and out of our lives offer us teachings constantly. They assist us in seeing the world from a different viewing point. While I lived on the island I found many such teachings in the wilds among the flora and fauna. I also met a woman who assisted me in putting some of my more recent experiences into perspective, allowing me to move forward with greater understanding.

Sharon and I owned businesses that were next door to one another in the hamlet of Langely. We met when I went into her store and noticed a calendar hanging on the wall. The picture on the calendar was of a large tree in a forest, much like the ones on the island. At the base of the tree was a rather large opening from which tiny lights emanated, like fairy lights. I looked at it and then said to Sharon, "I believe in that stuff. I see things like that all the time." I was referring to the internal structures and external lights and colors I had been *seeing* in and around people, plants and animals for the past 8 years or so. Sharon smiled. I then asked her if she knew anyone who did intuitive readings. She laughed and said, "I do." We talked for a while and scheduled a time in which she would share her gift with me.

The time arrived for our meeting and I went to Sharon's house. She sat me down and told me I was a healer, that I could *see*, and that I needed to get busy and direct that *seeing* ability so that I could allow this gift to expand to its fullest extent. I sat there, drowning in my own tears. That day the brush was internally cleared from my path and I have never looked back.

My work as a medical intuitive certainly addresses the physical problems and issues of clients and students. The label "medical intuitive," as most labels are, is a bit limiting in describing the work that I do. During a typical session, I move where the body directs me although not in any specific order:

- I systematically scan and discern what is going on within someone's body and its various systems — both physically, as well as etherically.
- I use the chakra system and the meridian acupuncture points as assessment tools and use them to apply corrective measures when appropriate.

- I check things such as bone density, all the major organs of the body as well as the systems they are attached to, i.e., pulmonary, cardiovascular, digestive, neurological (synaptic function), etc.
- I intuit the speed at which a client's body metabolizes and/or assimilates various foods and check nutritional balances.
- In addition, there are emotional and behavior components of disorders, misalignments and diseases that are addressed, as well as a multitude of relationships within a person's being.

Many clients ask how they should prepare for a session. Actually, there is nothing anyone has to do. I like to *read* them as they are, with no special dietary constraints attached. Some jokingly tell me that they'll watch what they eat before their appointment. It doesn't matter. If they are eating something that their body doesn't like, their body will tell me, even if it's been a number of days since they binged on their personal "forbidden fruit." A woman came to me for a reading and as I read the energy that was held within and around her pancreas, I asked when was the last time she had eaten a moderate to large amount of potato chips that were cooked in peanut oil. She looked surprised and said, "Four days ago. But how did you know?" Her body told me that it was still having trouble with the peanut oil as it was still detectable within her body.

I use my intuition beyond that of the label medical intuitive — although my life and work have often called me into that arena. Intuition allows me to pick up subtle biochemical imbalances as well as microscopic disorders within the body. I also intuit the emotional/behavioral components that surround the organs, soft tissue and bones of the body. In addition, when I work with cancer patients who are usually under a physician's care, there has been success in tracking the directional movement of the cancer and other diseases before a CAT or MRI can pick them up.

My work is based on the physiology of the body, yet, I address the soul and the issues that are screaming to come forth. In all cultures, the soul often uses the only voice that can be heard — discomfort and pain within the physical body.

More often than not, clients hear internal whisperings long before the disease arrives. It is when they are distressed, due to a disease that has been diagnosed or have been dealing with a chronic illness, that they finally make it to my door. The ability to see what is happening within their physical structure gives them a sense of peace that builds trust.

Once this trust has been established, I tell every client that they have the same abilities that I do. And, that you can do for yourself, and most likely for others, what I do. Once you establish trust, an inner knowing about who you are begins and opens the door to your soul. It is there, at a soul level, where the real work and healing begin. You are your own true healer.

2

The Soul

It is an evolutionary time on our planet and within our ever-widening global culture. It is time to embrace a state of mind that signals new levels of consciousness which bring about balance within the micro and macro cosmos of our existence. This call for balance comes to us in many forms. Being in service as a medical intuitive, I see many people wherein the subtle whispers from their bodies in the form of aches, pains or diseases are urging them to become more aware and enlightened regarding their interconnectedness to all things — energetically, physically and mentally.

Within the larger cultural context and the various institutions within the global community — political, economic, educational, religious, and familial — there is also a crying out for balance to be brought forth. It appears that we haven't been taking care of our human beingness. In order to do that, we need to step forward into a new way of living — a new way of being well.

It is time to take those steps, addressing the changes that are part of this natural evolutionary process of consciousness which is currently rising quietly and has risen before, in sometimes not so recognizable ways, within various global cultures throughout time. The time is at hand for us to join collectively in this upliftment. Collectively, because we are all one. The veils of illusion that have separated us are about to lift even further.

I was once on a airplane returning from Southeast Asia. As far as I could tell, I was the only white woman on the huge Boeing 747. I sat with closed eyes in the middle of this plane, seemingly the stranger in the crowd. Someone sneezed. It sounded just like one of my sneezes. We are all inherently the same and come from the same cosmic force. Outward appearances and illusions of polarity keep us from embracing our oneness and chain our perceptions to duality.

As you approach the various crossroads that lie on your pathway, it is true that this evolutionary process of con-sciousness is not always quiet within you. Upliftment can be tumultuous at time. Yet, it is time to shift, again. Supporting in a cyclical manner the micro and macro perspectives, our current way of living has created the anatomy of our individual lives and respective cultures. That again is true throughout time. Moreover, as you view current events, filled with their numerous structures and components, you can see that the culture is demanding that we pay attention to the result(s) of living within the old paradigms. These old paradigms seem to be crumbling. The fabric of the culture within and without is, indeed, orchestrating the timeless shifting of consciousness. It is up to you and to be aware, attentive and willing to address that which is destined to be.

As far as illness, misalignment and disease are concerned, it has become exceedingly clear, from my experience, that it is most certainly our way of living — our spiritual, mental and physical habits — that dictate our way of being. Furthermore, inclusive within that state of being and being human, lie our states of awareness. It is within these states of consciousness that our perceptions and beliefs reside, which include our mental and emotional thoughts regarding our health and wellness, or lack thereof.

When we come from a place of deep awareness and understanding regarding the proper care and wellness of the human being, we concurrently bring about change within the larger community. If this resonates for you, it is time to explore your own nature and embrace the eternal existence of the unified self and of our communal destiny. It may be time to consider redesigning how you care for your humanness.

There is a new call for internal/external awareness. These concepts regarding the calling forth of one's soulful nature have been illuminated since the beginning of time to varying degrees of prominence. Accomplishing this type of leap will require you to understand the depth and breadth of what is happening in both the interior and exterior arenas of your subjective world.

Natural protocols will be on your side, because as you make individualized shifts and garner new levels of awareness and consciousness, you will automatically and naturally join with others who are like-minded. This initiates a "group think" type of energy, which propels the collective toward a quantum leap in consciousness. It is all around us.

Television commercials and movies are flavored with nuances that indicate a culture moving toward a greater spiritual consciousness. Monastic chanting, images of ETs, spirits from the other side, and various intuitive and spiritual dialogues fill the airwaves and theaters. There is no mistaking that we have arrived at a marvelous, yet precarious, point in our evolution of consciousness. We are poised at a place in which we can learn to heal our world and ourselves, bringing about a level of wellness that is sustained by innate wisdom — intuition.

As we watch the paradigms shifting in and around us, we return, quite naturally to certain fundamental questions. Who am I? What is my life's purpose? Where did I come from? Why am I here? All of this shifting and changing is an organic process contained within a natural and universal set of protocols. When strife, suffering and change occur, we humans ultimately turn our search and childlike yearnings towards that which created us, or toward that which we are a part of, not apart from. We go there, if for no other reason to ask these types of questions — who, what, where and why. In reality, we all know what this feels like. We have all asked these questions with such heartfelt anguish that the battlefields made of human bones pale to the internal sense of insignificance that plays throughout our being. You wonder why you have a disease? Why someone you loved has died? Or why it hurts so much trying to fit in? Sufferings and woes seem steeped in ignorance and fueled by misalignment. Dysfunctional thoughts rage within. Biochemistry shifts in the body, ultimately taking causative postures and manifesting physical ailments.

Attempting to contend with these inner enemies is more often than not, tougher than any mortal foe you have encountered. Once you agree to become your own healer and find your internal surgical laser — which will be one of the tools you will develop while reading this book — the light will begin to shine and healing will begin to take place. Platform after platform upon which you have built your life and consciousness will lift higher. As a result of your inner work, you will no longer bury your ideas or surrender your voice to the paralyzed nature that seems common and fated.

To properly care for and feed your soul, which will set the stage for wellness within your human beingness, it is necessary to realize that all the aspects of who you are reflect the holographic nature of your soul. You are a soul — an essence of pure mind and heart that holds a specific vibration — whose destiny is, at some point within the boundlessness of time, to be filled with the pure light of consciousness — with the light of God. Given that on some level, you are already whole and perfect in God's eyes, no matter what has manifested in your life or in your physical body. As well, you will know when you are about to embark on a journey that will lead you through the process of self-discovery (realization of your connection to God) and then onward into self-mastery (actualization of the God within you).

Take note of these three words. Whole, Who and Hole. Within the word whole you will see the word who — meaning of course that within the whole of the universe there you are — the who. Also, within the whole exist the holes through which you, as a personality that is gaining in conscious awareness, can see, feel, hear, or know the areas of your personality and mind's consciousness that are here to evolve and grow. In short, you will discover through these holes that pop up occasionally in your life the issues that your spirit, mind and body will be dealing with during this lifetime. Moreover, they allow you to experience the areas of growth that are demanded of your soul to bring it eventually into alignment with the pure mind of God — the whole. Rest assured that there is a part of you that is already whole and perfectly enlightened. Yet, make no mistake about it: all of the things that you have experienced in your life thus far have been opportunities for you to grow. You can look back upon your past opportunities and see the truth woven through them. Your soul, and its desire to help your personality evolve. It has been escorting you through the vast experiences of your life's banquet, using your emotions to breathe form into your experience(s) as well as placing them firmly into your spirit, mind and body's anatomy. It is your job to become aware of this process and manage it consciously through choice and free will, not willfulness, and to bring about the liberation of your soul. It is up to you to release your soul, mind and body from various levels of pain, ignorance and suffering.

It's important that you go beyond the first-blush meanings of these words so that you understand the concepts, energies and essences that lie behind them. You will, through the reading and doing of this book, discover the universal energy that brings all things into being and assures your growth and evolution. The shift will happen for you as it has for thousands of students. Your overall awareness of life will begin to unfold to deeper levels. Intuitive, mental and physical wellness will unfurl as well. You will experience, to varying degrees based on your dedication and your practice, a truer sense of self and, therefore, become enraptured as realizations reveal the eternity of your being.

It is your job to become as aware as you can and listen, in an absorbing manner, deep within to find your guidance. It is your job, as well, to find that place of even-mindedness within your emotional being that will ultimately foster and bring about inner knowing and peace. This place of peace will be delivered unto you, through your practice and in that place of even-mindedness in which you do not swing from one end of the emotional pendulum to the other.

Receiving Your Invitation
to a New Way of Living

In the past when I would teach Intuitive Therapeutics, a healing modality I developed along my path, I had made it a practice never to tell students what exactly would demonstrate in their life when they did their homework — some of the work that is laid out in this book. I would share potentialities, but did not necessarily give past student examples of actualized change. However, one night a student changed my mind regarding this policy. It was the third of four classes that were spaced two weeks apart and the students were beginning their fifth week of exercises. As always, I held a check-in time at the beginning of class to see how everyone was doing.

Hannah raised her hand and laughingly said to me, "How come you didn't tell us that this class would change our lives?" I told her that after committing to this type of work, I had always seen profound changes in people and their lives. In the past, I hadn't said anything because I didn't want to program the students. I wanted everyone to have his or her own experience without any kind of expectation. Hannah then told me that she was OK with the fact that her life had changed so dramatically since she had started taking the course and doing the exercises, but wished that I had told her just how much her life was about to change. She then told us how she had spent five days with her best friend of the last 12 years and that within their time together she realized that now she had nothing in common with this woman. She was surprised at the realization of how much the class work had caused shifts and changes in her.

Hannah didn't know what to do or what to say to her friend. All she knew was that she was somehow different. She understood more clearly than she had ever understood before what served her in her life and what didn't. Through her new dedication to her spiritual practice and experiences with the class's exercises, she had gained a deeper understanding of what she needed to move within her life's environment. It was a powerful moment for her. She then owned who she was and what she wanted to become, realizing that placation and appeasement would no longer be a part of her life. No longer would she stay in a relationship, any relationship, that didn't move her toward growth.

I'd been working with James for quite a while. It was a privilege to assist him in moving through some deep early childhood scars and wounds, however, his issues regarding control over things that he could not control were still present. His energetic heart center (chakra) was closed down to a larger degree than he wanted, affecting his feelings about everything and everyone in his life. He wanted to change, but was stuck.

I was concerned that there was nothing more I could do for him as he traveled through this particular cycle in his life. The energy around his heart had concretized. One day, as I worked with him, I placed my hand on his heart's energetic center and the impact of energy was so strong regarding the buildup of congestion that it affected a vein in my hand which remained bruised for several days. That was the last time I saw James, but my prayers for him continued. In August of the same year, I got a call from his wife saying that he had been rushed to the hospital with heart problems and they had just placed a stent in his artery. Our work began again.

Today James is a different man, and he will never be the same. His heart, the loving gentle heart space he came into this world with, has been reborn, and all aspects of his life — physical, emotional, and mental — are healing. His eyes shine every time I see him and my heart wells up with joy for James and his family. It took a life-threatening situation for him to finally understand that controlling things and people around him in order to feel safe was moving him through life in a way that was unhealthy. He also realized through facing his own mortality that no one should have to go through what he did in order to "get it." He is now an inspiration to others around him.

James had been and will always be a special client and friend. He had the courage to look within and stare directly into his fears. From there, he was able to understand them and release them. Consequently, his process took him to new and fertile fields of consciousness, wellness and inner peace.

It is not my intention in the classroom, in the office or in this book to prevent anyone from following his or her path — particularly when it holds the most growth. Nevertheless, if I can support someone in the understanding of their soul's existence and, more importantly, assist them in discovering what messages are trapped within their body's physical and energetic structure, then my intention is met.

Here is a little lesson my father shared with me while I was visiting my parents' home in Ohio over the holidays years ago. The story demonstrates an intention behind the giving of oneself in service to others. My father often carried his dog Fritzie around in his arms like an infant. I was intrigued by him doing this, so I teasingly told my father, "Daddy, Fritzie can walk, you know." My father stopped, nuzzled his face up against Fritzie's muzzle, looked at me with his angelic eyes and said most proudly, "Yes, Fritzie can walk. But isn't it nice that he doesn't have to?"

I laughed — the message was received in regard to service toward others. Moreover, I do so firmly believe that you can, indeed, discover, learn and heal, bringing about your own state of wellness by yourself. Nonetheless, even though you can walk through your own labyrinth, there are those time when we all need a little assistance and guidance from an outside source to which we can turn. That is what my prayer is — to be there for someone if they need a little help. There is a Buddhist vow which, in part, states, "May I be a protector for all who need one. May I be a ship, a boat, a raft for all who wish to cross the water..." To act in this manner, as a vessel or catalyst, in order to assist another person to cross the waters of life is a wonderful way of being. It is a way of being that will serve humanity. We are all one; therefore, when you help another, you are truly helping yourself as well.

I want to share with you this: Yes, you can walk. Yes, you can do your own healing, or at least be in charge of the healing team you have gathered around you. And when you need a little help, you will find others around you who will hold you dearly in their arms. As well, what excites me is that the time is right now. Consciousness levels within the human race are awakening at rapid speeds. Synchronistic events, which are indications of more personal awareness regarding the interconnection of life on a larger scale, are becoming more prominent to the masses. Those who have been more pursuant of a spiritual path are reaching even greater heights of consciousness. Perhaps you can catch on more easily than I did. You don't have to wait to receive a more physically demanding predicament to initiate your soul's growth.

You can simply begin now — start the process of uncovering your soul's voice and bring forth your intuitive, mental and physical wellness. Perhaps it is lost under issues that you have been unwilling to look at honestly. A brilliant young woman named Sally came to me for assistance in correcting her vision. Studying to be a doctor, her schedule was a bit hectic. We made some initial progress in the first session or two which allowed her to go without the use of her glasses for a short period of time. She went without them because her vision had cleared. She believed with all her heart that she could see again without the aid of glasses, and she believed this because she had experienced clear vision spontaneously prior to seeing me and then again after I had worked with her.

Sally came in for another appointment and I suggested that she needed to look at some emotional issues. It was my understanding, as I read the thought forms within her body's tissue and within her energy field as well, that there were some deep emotional scars that needed healing in order for her eyesight to stay in a corrective pattern. In short, in order to see, Sally needed to look at things in her life she hadn't been able to look at truthfully. Sally acknowledged that there were some deep-seated emotional issues from childhood, but due to her medical school schedule she simply didn't want to stir up her emotional pot, so to speak, right then.

I was sympathetic to her reasons, but was direct in my assessment that healing must take place in the heart (her emotional eyes) as well as in her physical eyes. The results after this session were less dramatic, if not nonexistent. I haven't seen Sally since, but send her healing when she appears in my mind's eye. In any case, she will at some point in time look at these issues, and will be an even greater doctor than she could ever imagine.

This brings up an important point. You are your own healer. With that being said, you need to be willing to heal, on all levels. When I speak of levels here, I am referring to emotional, physical, mental, spiritual and those that you may not know by name. Levels of consciousness that lie somewhere beyond in a nameless place.

People frequently want to give their healing powers away to someone, anyone. A client named Beth came to me from out of town. She was suffering from adrenal depletion and all that accompanies it. On our third visit, she told me that an intuitive back East had told her that when she came to Arizona she would meet a woman, but that woman was not really a woman. She was an angel disguised as a woman. Beth's eyes began to well up with tears and she then said, "You're that angel. I just know it." I was honored by her comments, however, I know who Beth's true healer is.

We proceeded with the session. Beth was lying quietly on the healing table and I had my hand underneath her, moving the energy in her adrenal area. I began to playfully dialogue quietly with God. Well, God, I said, if I'm such an angel, why can't I instantly heal this woman? (Now I know very well that I am only a healing facilitator. Yet, I become frustrated over the suffering that goes on in clients. I do pray that I could heal them instantly, even though I know clearly that the lessons they need to learn are not in the healing, they are in the journey toward the healing.) After making such an outspoken comment to God, I heard a voice booming, in a sideways direction, through my head and mind. "Angels are messengers. Just messengers. Healing is between her soul and God!" I stayed there prayerfully moving energy through Beth's body, reminded of my place and my role: the messenger, or reporter, as I call it.

Healing occurs on a variety of consciousness levels and it is true that consciousness levels are many. A prayer I hold for humankind is that we evolve and arrive at a deeper understanding of who we are and how we are connected to the whole. However, many people do cross over without having once tasted the sweet nectar of their soul, which is the ultimate connection with consciousness and with the God (in his/her many forms) within us all. Nonetheless, as demonstrated by these few examples, it should always be understood that any and all healing is guided by the will of the seeker, wrapped in their karma and the will of God or Spirit.

This illustration depicts another soul's journey from which we can all graciously learn. Neil was a very charming man and had everything going for him in his life. At least it appeared that way on the surface. He was a powerful, internationally-recognized businessman, with a beautiful wife and two intelligent young boys poised to follow in his footsteps. He had all the trappings that come with success within the Western definition. Neil came to see me through the advice of a mutual friend after he was diagnosed with 18 brain tumors and a spot on his lung. Needless to say, he was scared and consequently very willful. He did not want to die. He was not going to die. It was simply not in his life's plan of action — which he had laid out in a literal step-by-step format that helped manage both his personal and professional life's goals, allowing him to obtain what he desired.

When I scanned his body it became clear that the cancer was extremely aggressive in nature — much like his nature when it came to business and the control he exerted in his life. Neil and his wife told me that he had just had an MRI so they knew the location of the cancerous tumors and were using radiation to combat the disease. Even though I knew the locations of the tumors, I sensed there was more to the picture.

God has blessed all of us with varying levels of inner sight — intuition. It can be honed to the degree that the seer can detect and sense the directional movement of diseases such as cancer. This inner sight can be called upon to be molecularly oriented, so as to sense and see the particles of the molecular structure that are beginning to formulate and have the potential to manifest into physical form. Based on this way of seeing, I discovered that the directional movement of Neil's cancer was rapidly heading down his spinal cord and lymphatic system and would soon be manifested in his legs. I worked on him for about an hour and through the modulation of energy, several hurtful issues were brought to the surface along with equally deeply buried tears. We scheduled another appointment and Neil and his wife left my office.

Part of my spiritual practice is that at the end of the day I go into mediation after I see all my clients. From that meditative state, I send prayers and do remote work on anyone who has requested it. Because of my appointment with Neil, I was deeply moved by his desires to be cured. I felt, however, in addition to his desires for a cure, there needed to be some deep healing.

Sitting within the silence of myself, I asked for guidance as to how I could be of service to Neil and his family. What I received was a startling vision of an angel, holding a clipboard. Although, it sounds rather bizarre, experience has taught me to trust spirit-guided knowledge and phenomena, as it often demonstrates in ways in which we can translate and/or understand it more easily. So there, standing before me, within my mind's eye, was a beautiful angel holding a clipboard. The message, which was the response to my question, was quick and clear. "No, time is up. Early November." And with the statement, the angel took a pen and put a check mark on the clipboard, no doubt by Neil's name.

I felt helpless. Based on my vision, coupled with the intuitive information I had gleaned from my reading regarding the aggressiveness of the cancer and its directional movement, it was clear that his time was up. All I could do was to support him and his family in whatever way they wanted. Even with this decisive information and clear vision, I still held the space open for that lightning bolt of a miracle to take place. Such as I could, I assisted Neil based on my own illness and deathlike experience, as I knew what it felt like to die of a disease — the fears, the searing pain, etc. I also understood where he was and where he was going — even though this time I was watching from the outside someone else's suffering and pain.

Neil was willful, and he fought his cancer to his very last breath. To him the cancer was a mistake. He never really opened the invitation for his soul's growth or read between the lines of his life. He never owned the way he was living through his choices. He never owned his emotions, or the pain he had been holding inside of him for years. He died with his consciousness still holding the pain and suffering. It will undoubtedly release sometime, as the work regarding our soul's evolution continues on after we leave this world. The task here in this life on earth is to clean up as much as possible, because we take those emotions with us and still have to deal with them, sooner or later.

There is good news, however, regarding receiving invitations to your soul's evolution — you do not necessarily have to get hit over the head with God's velvet hammer. You do not necessarily need to go to the extremes of illness and teasing death to get the picture. Invitations for you to move into deeper levels of awareness, wellness and opportunities for your personal growth can come in very simple ways.

For instance, while giving a lecture at a bookstore several years ago I noticed a young woman who sat smiling through the entire program. As my lecture concluded, she raised her hand and announced that she had to tell the story of how she got to the lecture that evening. Her name was Juliet and she said that she had been out driving around looking for a new apartment when something inside of her told her to go into the bookstore and get a cup of coffee. The interesting thing is that she could have stopped for a cup of coffee at a number of other places. Nonetheless, her soul's voice was whispering to her, and through her intuition told her to "go to that bookstore to get a cup of coffee."

Juliet went on to explain that as soon as she entered the store, the public address system announced my lecture and the topic I was going to discuss. She went on to say that she had recently received several books from a friend on this particular topic. All of which was why she sat through the entire program grinning from ear to ear. Juliet knew that she had been led and guided into this store by that voice deep within her — her intuition. She had listened, paid attention and didn't have to get hit over the head to step into a new level of awareness.

It is totally up to you as to how you choose to listen and commit to your wisdom, or not. Your intuition is a powerful tool that can be sharpened and honed to the point that you can rely on and trust it within the daily context of your life. It is up to you to open up and begin to trust what you are getting intuitively. My prayer is that you take this simple tool, a tool you were born with, and work with it, develop it and commit to its use. Your life will change.

My desire is that, through these attendant exercises, you will begin to know the interconnectedness within you and grasp your connection to the creator and all things. The exercises in this book, and the application of them to your life and to your life's learning, makes for an interesting jigsaw puzzle. You may know this already. Nonetheless, these exercises will help you move into a more spiritual and/or intellectual understanding. They will also assist you in moving into a greater sense of body awareness. When it gets in your body, the densest part of yourself, you've got it.

3

Energy:
The Fire of Spirit, Mind
and Body

In this section and throughout the book I will use the word energy quite often. I want you to understand, however, when I speak of energy I am referring to two very distinct and important qualities. First, energy is a byproduct or commodity of consciousness. In this context, energy is the demonstration of consciousness in a more dense, yet subtle form. Secondly, energy is more palpable than consciousness. For instance, when someone says something to you and you feel goose bumps or a sour stomach, you are being impacted by their consciousness. You are feeling their consciousness demonstrate more physically as energetic sensations within your body. Energetic impact(s) on your body create stimulation of both your neurological and biochemical systems, whereby affecting even grosser levels of matter within your body — muscles, organ tissues and bone structure. The exercises in this book will help you feel your energy. I simply want you to be aware that what you are feeling are levels of consciousness, thought forms, that are residing in and around your physical body.

Within your body, you have an interconnected system of subtle lines and vortices of energy which both emanate from and support the denser molecular matter of your physical body. These lines or channels of energy are called nadis (pronounced 'na-dees) and the vortices are called chakras ('cha-kras). Each of the primary chakras has a specific color and level of consciousness. Please remember that what I am describing to you is only a standardized model and you, as an individual, will not necessarily follow a standard model to the letter. Thank goodness for the uniqueness of you.

Therefore, as you engage in working with your chakras and begin to experience them you may see, feel, hear or know a color or certain thought form(s) of consciousness moving through your body's awareness. Again, what you experience may jog away from the standard and I want you to recognize that it is perfectly fine to sense this variety within you. Simply be in the place of the observer and allow it all to happen. These variances are due to the fact that the chakras are extraordinarily interconnected, and therefore, reflect your common issues, energies as well as levels of consciousness and behavior within your energetic system — the chakras and nadis.

For example, you may have a survival issue, which is a first chakra (root chakra) consciousness, caught up in and connected to your fifth (throat chakra) or third (solar plexus/stomach) chakra. In short you may have a fear, worry or concern that is connected to the way in which you survive (first chakra) on this planet and it is difficult for you to express (throat chakra) this issue or move forward in a self-confident manner (solar plexus/stomach chakra).

When I look at a person, I see a myriad of colors emanating from their physical body, swirling and dancing in a kaleidoscope-like manner. You will probably be able to note these occurrences as you develop your intuitive sense more fully. Please note that the energies within and without the physical body indicate many things. Two of which are that the body's energy always tells the truth of a situation, and in that truthful telling, the process and the causation for a particular pattern of energy, or its consequences, are never black and white issues. Your body's current and past physical structure, its attendant energies, as well as your behaviors, emotions, current and potential levels of consciousness are all enfolded and wrapped within your life's experiences. Therefore, these experiences are reflected in the variances of color throughout your chakra system and your body's surrounding energy field.

In actuality, there are 350 chakras on the body and a highway system of 72,000 nadis (energy channels) which assist in the flow of energy, prana (subtle life-force energy), throughout both your energetic and physical bodies. For the purpose of this work, however, we will be focusing on the seven primary chakras, which will be delineated later.

On a physical body level the chakras play an invaluable role in maintaining balance within the body. This is the impetus of energy medicine and the work attendant therein. So many people are moving through their life with tired and worn out bodies. This is due, in part, to the fact that the chakras have a notable relationship and effect on the endocrine system of the body. When your body is stimulated by an energetic impact, the next along the energetic/physical continuum, so to speak, is the neurological system. The neurological system of the body is the closest to the energetic system in the sense that one could qualify them both by saying that they are electrically-based to some degree. The body system that is next affected by neurological impulses is the endocrine system. The ductless glands of the endocrine system as well as the neurological system are the physical, internal directors that maintain control and balance within the body. The neurological and the endocrine system are self-regulating. They align and continually realign the body and mind as they are stimulated with both internal and external forms of stimulation — energetic impacts.

Even the tiniest imbalance in the energetic system affects the neurological and endocrine systems, and are stimuli for hormones to flood into your blood stream from the endocrine system. Science has shown us that hormones can alter moods, behaviors which can direct motivation and even one's physical appearance. Also, hormones stimulate and alter bodily functions such as respiration and digestion. The endocrine system is extraordinarily influential in regards to our body/mind function. Literally, your zest and vitality for life is affected by this system. Even your intellectual abilities can be altered based on hormonal secretions within your body. Given all of this, it is essential for you to gain both understanding and experience(s) regarding the importance and impact, inner workings and expressions of your energetic system, as well as the results exhibited on your physical health and wellness.

The Seven Primary Chakras

In this section, the seven primary chakras will be briefly described, I will share with you the chakra, its location, what physiology it affects, as well as a client example which will demonstrate the application of the chakra model in reference to real life situations. As you are guided throughout this book, getting aquatinted with your own energy system through experiential exercises, you will learn to see, feel, hear, smell and/or know how to open, balance and cleanse your chakras. The methods with which you will experience your energetic system are time-tested and come from ancient wisdom — wisdom that goes beyond this lifetime, having been plucked from the consciousness of the mind stream wherein lies all knowledge.

As you will note, chakra one (located at the tailbone) and chakra seven (located at the crown of the head) simply

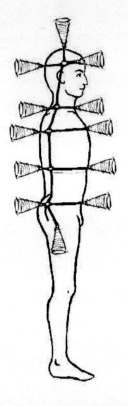

7th Chakra - violet purple
6th Chakra - indigo

5rd Chakra - sky blue
4th Chakra - green
3rd Chakra - yellow

2nd Chakra - orange

1st Chakra - red

leave the body in a downward and upward direction respectively. Chakras two, three, four, five and six all have a front and back. Nonetheless, each chakra is made from the same atomic structure that your physical body is made from. In fact, it is the same atomic structure from which all life is constructed. However, since the chakras are subtle constructs of energy, their mass is less dense and therefore, cannot be seen by the naked eye. Training and practice in developing your intuition, or heightened sensitivities, through your intuitive learning preference(s) of *seeing, hearing, feeling, smelling or knowing* will allow you to have tangible and traceable experiences with your chakras.

Each chakra's etheric form is attached to the physical spinal column in the body — hence its direct effect of the neurological system and all other systems of the body. In the way in which I perceive the chakras there is a contact lens-like structure that is connected to both the physical spine and to the nonphysical chakra. The energetic structure and density of this lens lie somewhere between physical form and nonphysical form, similar to the way in which water vapor that is not yet mist, steam or fog lies between the density of air and of water. The molecules of water are present within the vapor, yet they cannot be seen as of yet by the naked eye. You need a device to detect them. Your intuition is the device that will allow you to detect your energetic system. Again, that is why it is imperative for you to develop a heightened state of awareness. (Remember, energy and life are not black and white and there are many dimensions available to us.)

It is this lens-like structure that acts as both a conduit and an interpreter. It transfers energetic stimuli from its external source, through and from the aqueous of energy that surrounds your body, into one or more chakras. From the chakra(s), the stimulus penetrates more deeply, moving through this contact-lens like structure, after which it moves into the denser neurological system held within the spinal column, spreading the energies throughout your system. The directional spreading of this energy is often determined by the emotional components and intentions that are encoded in the stimulus that was transferred to you. The feeling of butterflies or uneasiness in your stomach is your body's electrochemical and emotional reaction to outside energetic stimulation hitting that particular energetic center. In this case, it is your solar plexus. These types of impacts, consisting of energetics and thought forms, can leave quite an impression on your spirit, body and mind. I will discuss these types of impacts later in the book.

The first chakra is located at the tailbone of the spinal column. The color is red and the primary consciousness attached to the first chakra is that of survival. Purely and simply, the first chakra is about the foundational consciousness that dictates how we survive within the context of this life. It is the foundational consciousness/energy upon which all other chakras are built. Releasing unhealthy attachments to societal conditions regarding "how to survive" are essential in order to gain higher levels of consciousness and truly feel the interconnectedness of God within your entire being, as well as with all other beings.

In addition to the primal force which perpetuates the consciousness of procreation, driving us to survive as a species, we may attach a variety of culturally-based thought forms — consciousnesses — as to how we can survive. Insecurities are born, so to speak, in the first chakra, even though they may be connected to another chakra (psychophysical/emotional consciousness center). For example, you may feel a strong need to conform to every whim and fad society has to offer in order to survive, to feel safe or to feel included. Conversely, you may be more prone to an iconoclastic manner of being and feel a need to be as far removed from societal pressures as you can in order to survive. You, like others around you, may attach yourself to concepts of money, having a mate or the need to be close to family. As well, you can have attachments to living in certain regions of the world, or in a particular environment. Any situation in which you demonstrate behavioral patterns, language (verbal or nonverbal) and emotions regarding survival issues incorporates first chakra consciousness and energy.

On a physiological level, the first chakra influences the tailbone, the coccyx area of the spinal column, as well as the legs, colon (large intestine), prostrate, perineum and any other tissue and/or bodily structure within that section of the body. Have you ever been or know of someone who has been in a fearful situation and the colon quickly emptied? That physiological function demonstrates the fear of survival — a first chakra issue. The colon emptying out quickly is a signal from the first chakra transferred into the neurological system that the foundational structure of your being is being changed or challenged in some way. You feel a loss of control and your body responds accordingly.

First chakra consciousness is geared to body level consciousness. Moreover, the first chakra is strongly attached to this perceived hard reality that is third dimensional in nature. First chakra issues deal with physical foundational issues around our structures. The various levels of fear, worry or concern residing within you will dictate, to a large degree, the level of risk that you are willing to take in your life. As well, based on your subconscious or conscious levels of perception regarding survival, the first chakra will reveal your attachment(s) to other people, places or things and whether they are fear-based perceptions or not. It is an important and revealing arena of consciousness and energy to look at within yourself. As within all of the chakra centers, hidden truths will arise, and if blessed and released, will set you free, detaching you from that which does not serve your consciousness, energy, body or your way of life.

Georgia, a beautiful and talented woman, came to see me with severe anxiety. Georgia was under the guidance of a doctor and was taking some medications which were to assist her in relieving her anxiety and some that were to help her sleep at night. She described her unsettling family situation as she was growing up and it was clear that her first chakra was lighting up as a major point of energetic congestion — holding emotional pain. She was fearful. We talked at length and I reported to her what her body was telling me — fear around abandonment, not speaking her truth and fear about moving forward with her talents. Georgia had been trained as an operatic singer, and when she spoke of her voice and her singing, her body and facial features lit up so beautifully. I sensed in her the desire to allow herself to sing once more.

At the close of our time together we talked about her fears that had been so prevalent in her life. Interestingly enough, Georgia had lost her tailbone in an accident. This is an important point, given the fact that in energy medicine the root chakra, the chakra that governs and supports foundational/survival energy, was missing from her physiology. In energy medicine, there is a connection between the missing tailbone, the damage to the root chakra, the disheveled way in which her childhood was, the building of anxiety she had been experiencing and the peak of her emotional state now. Even through she could not replace the tailbone, she could compensate with concentrated focus of energy in that area to heal and rebalance it. That rebalancing would have a trickle-down effect toward the more mental, emotional and physical struggles Georgia was facing as well.

The second chakra is located in the abdominal area of the physical body. The standard color of the second chakra is orange. The primary consciousness governed by the second chakra is that of sexual, creative energy which governs our concepts and perceptions regarding relationships of all manner of speaking. Everything we objectively manifest within our third dimensional reality is born from second chakra sexual, creative energy, no matter if it is the birth of a baby, an idea, career path, our income, our friendships, partnerships or other type of relationship to the world in and around us. All of these are born of second chakra energy.

On a body level, the second chakra energy governs the reproductive organs, the pelvic structures, both muscular and skeletal, as well as all other tissues attendant in that area of the body. The endocrine system plays an important role in the second chakra, governing reproductive and various hormonal functions as well as certain digestive processes. Many of the disorders and diseases, both physical and emotional, are born from conflicting, dysfunctional perceptions regarding the proper care and feeding of your second chakra creative, sexual energy and consciousness.

In my day-to-day practice, I see so much abuse regarding the giving and taking of second chakra energy. It is rampant throughout the world and is culturally specific regarding the way in which it manifests. Yet no one, in any culture, is exempt from these types of abuses. People are giving away or having their second chakra energy taken from them all the time in unbalanced ways and to varying degrees. These can include areas such as dysfunctional sexual issues and behaviors in both men and women. Many men and women in the work place are drained on a daily basis of their creative energy by feeling the pressure to perform and create. This is especially taxing when you don't really like what you are doing for your vocation, nor the people who you are working with and/or for. There is nothing more deadly than being in an environment in which you are forced to create and push yourself to the brink of exhaustion and illness.

In the healing facilitation work that I do, I see so many parts of the body thrown out of whack due to the stress of misused energy, especially second chakra energy. For a simplistic example, if you have chronic lower back pain, simply be open enough to take a look at whether or not you are always using your creative energy in a forceful manner. That forceful manner can manifest in a personality that feels that they always have to fix everybody, and that it is their job to create the perfect home or office, child or project. Naturally, not all lower back problems result from these few examples. I mention them simply to get you thinking of how you use your body's energy, second chakra creative consciousness and the connection to your emotions, behaviors and perceptions.

The back of the chakras dictate the willpower that is moved through that particular chakra to accomplish the ideal dictated by the chakras consciousness. The example above regarding using your will to create, at times places undue stress and force on the back of the second chakra. Any time you try to push through things that are not flowing well, using your will instead of letting your energy create space, places stress on the back of a chakra. To use the second chakra for an example: trying to force a creative resolution to a situation instead of letting the ideas flow in and through you is using the back of your second chakra energy — the will of your creative, sexual energy. This can throw the lumbar area of your spinal column out of whack, let alone what it can do to your internal organs in the lower abdominal region of your body if you continue to behave in that manner. Take a moment and think about how you use your will and where the locations are in your body that express occasional or chronic pain. Just be with the wisdom you gain.

Reproductive system diseases, in both males and females, are usually filled with the emotions of sadness, remorse, revenge, hatred, and downright exhaustion regarding the misuse of second chakra energy(ies). I have seen too many reproductive systems turned upside down, energetically speaking. Ovaries, uteruses and their surrounding tissues seethe with cysts, fibroids and cancers due to the sometimes hidden, yet, constantly repeated subconscious and conscious thought forms that women recite to themselves regarding the distracted, dysfunctional and the unbalanced giving away of their second chakra energy.

Just to give you an idea how powerful your perceptions and behaviors are, as well as the way they affect second chakra energy, I'll share this account with you. Sheila came to my office after having tried expensive fertility drugs and procedures in order to get pregnant. She came with the hope of finding out what was blocking her emotionally and/or energetically, if anything.

The first picture I saw within my mind's eye was Sheila at the age of seven or so. She was standing with her arms across her chest in defiance. She was angry with her mother, as the emotional energy of anger was attached to her mother's energy. In addition, her uterus, energetically had taken on the same posture. Within my mind's eye I saw that, energetically speaking, her uterus had turned itself around and wouldn't face her mother or, more accurately, the issues from this portion of her childhood. Furthermore, within her auric field, which is the aqueous of energy surrounding and supporting the physical body, I saw a light-filled energy mass in which the density of molecules   indicated   to   me   something   that   I   had felt   and   seen   before.   That   energetic   mass was that of her unborn child's soul or consciousness. It was there, floating outside her physical body within the auric field, waiting for Sheila to clear the issues around her mother so this soul could come into her body, and into her life. These three, Sheila, the husband and the child, had a contract to fulfill, and the child's soul was hanging around waiting for it to be fulfilled. I shared with my client what I was seeing and sensing then I proceeded to apply corrective measures — energy modulation — to this specific and other related areas of her body. She left my office. I got a call several weeks later saying that she was pregnant.

The third chakra resides in the area of the solar plexus, or stomach area of the body. The color is yellow. The physiology that is governed by the third chakra is the stomach, liver, gall bladder, pancreas, kidneys, adrenal glands and the other organs, tissues, muscles and skeletal structures within the midsection of the body. The consciousness of the third chakra is about power and will (different than the will associated with back of the chakras). The will that I am referring to regarding third chakra energy and consciousness is that of human will power that drives a person's concept of self. It is regarding self-esteem, self-worth, self-confidence and the overall empowerment of the self, or the lack of one or more of these. Interestingly enough there are powerful lymphatic glands in the third chakra region. In fact, that chakra's etheric cone-like structure runs right through a large physical lymph node. No wonder the lymphatic system and immune system of one's body can become compromised if it is constantly experiencing negative impacts of energy in that chakra region. Think about it. Have you ever been ill after being fired, dumped by a partner or any other situation in which your self-worth, self-esteem or power was stripped from you?   Have you ever held on to fear, worry or concern regarding your sense of self and self-esteem with such intensity that your stomach became upset or tense?

Gloria called me when she found out that she had pancreatic cancer. I went to see her and work with her while she was in the hospital. The cancer was rather aggressive, and it was clear to me she had a fight on her hands. Her loved ones told me as we conversed out in the hallway that she had always been afraid of dogs. Guess what. While she was in the hospital, a seeing-eye dog with its trainer holding the leash poked its head into her room. Gloria was terrified. Especially when the German Shepherd jumped up on the bed with her. According to her family and friends, the dog was like an angel in disguise and was surprisingly loving and gentle with Gloria.

After a few minutes Gloria started to calm down as she realized that this was a gift for her to finally rid herself of this fear. I was told that Gloria and the dog cuddled for quite some time. The whole experience called her to maneuver through her labyrinth of fear. Gloria later transitioned from her cancer. Nonetheless, her ability to face her fears, no matter how large or small, allowed her to gain some wisdom and understanding about her life and her process. Like Gloria, no matter where you are, no matter what your circumstances, sooner or later you will have to step up and face your fears and reclaim your power.

The fourth chakra is located in the center of the Thoracic region of the body. The color is green. The consciousness that governs the heart chakra is that of unconditional love which is pure and multidimensional in nature. That type of love is unlike the more one dimensional love/energy of sexual or romantic love. It is unconditional love that carries with it the potential for the divine romance between God and all of creation to occur within each and every one of us.

The heart chakra region, on a physiological level governs the lungs, ribs, heart, thymus gland as well as all muscles, tissues and skeletal structures within the thorax. I have always found it fascinating that I usually sense if, how and how long a person wants to live on this planet by tuning into or placing my hand upon their thymus gland. Pictures flow through my mind's eye and feeling nature as to the ease with which they are living their life. Both the difficulties and joy of how their life has unfolded, and whether or not it has unfolded into their heart's desire is indicated in this region of the body. Next time you are confused about which direction to take in your life, simply breathe in and out slowly and deeply into the heart chakra region. Place either hand over your chest and listen. Feel, see and sense with your own inner vision the direction(s) you are being told.

The heart chakra is, as well, the bridge chakra, through which the energy of the lower three chakras and the upper three chakras are linked. The heart chakra is the place where all of your chakras' voices can commune to be heard. Take the time to listen occasionally. It will undoubtedly change your life.

Julia, a giving, service-oriented woman, had recently changed careers. All her life she had given to others — her family, church, schools, business and community. When she retired from her life's work, which she had dearly loved, her life slowed down enough for her body to relay some very important messages to her. Within 18 months Julia went through breast cancer and a mastectomy, heart surgery (a triple by-pass) and her thyroid went into atrophy, nearly killing her. Her body, particularly her heart chakra, had been screaming at her to love herself as much as she had loved and cared for others. It was a powerful, poignant time in her life.

There is nothing wrong with giving service to others. I believe that is what we are here to do. However, to love and give to oneself as joyously as you give to others releases the resentments that can build up over time as you negate your own heart's desires in lieu of other's wants and needs. Besides, if you constantly give of yourself to others, without taking the time to replenish your own body, energy and sense of self, there won't be anything left of yourself with which to give service. This is a challenge for many women. It is also a challenge for those who don the hat of a healer. It is a lesson that will be learned, one way or another, sooner or later. It is easier if you start listening to your body and heart's whispers before it starts screaming at you.

Unconditional love, spiritual love, divine love, partnership love, etc. are all part of the relational love(s) that are brought forth, nurtured, stroked and sometimes dashed and trashed through this chakra center. If you are a human being and have walked on this planet for more than a few years, you have felt both the exhilarating explosion of and the suppression of heart chakra energy. As humans we spend an enormous amount of time and energy trying to find, keep, hold and nurture the love we desire. Luckily, most of us have an abundance of love to give, as it is part of innate nature to love and to be loved.

The love of God, along with the love of self and others in an honoring and compassionate way, is a powerful way to be and will open your heart center, allowing you to experience amazing levels of bliss, compassion and satisfaction for living. Loving gratitude is real power which, when held honestly within the heart chakra, within the center of your being, will magnetize all that is good and joyful unto you.

The fifth chakra is located at the throat. The color is sky blue. The consciousness that is governed by the throat chakra is that of communication, divine communication and truth. The main lesson for the human personality and the throat chakra is that of communicating the truth — speaking your truth to yourself and to others.

The physiology governed by the throat chakra are the thyroid, parathyroid, esophagus, larynx, pharynx, nose and sinuses. As well, the mouth, teeth, the salivary glands, and the components of the upper section of the alimentary canal are all governed by the fifth chakra.

Cynthia learned, up close and personal, what effect and power fifth chakra consciousness holds within it. Years ago, when she was married, she and her husband decided to purchase a business together in Cynthia's hometown. Prior to opening up this business Cynthia and her family needed to move there. So her husband quit his job, a job that he was unhappy with, and Cynthia abandoned her pursuit of a college degree. The couple put their house on the market, pulled their children out of school to move to Cynthia's hometown and purchase an existing business.

In their first eight months the business did very well. There was community acceptance and praise, and the financial end was promising. However, after the summer season had ended, Cynthia's husband decided he was not happy and wanted to move back. After much deliberation she caved in. Cynthia didn't speak out. She didn't speak her truth. She was afraid to. More often than not, whenever she attempted speak up her words were often met with anger and hateful words from her husband. Cynthia remained quiet. Her husband moved on beforehand to start a new job and she was left with the tasks of selling the business, a home which she and the children dearly loved, pulling the children out of school again and moving back with her husband.

Months passed. Cynthia was very angry inside and as a result of not feeling safe enough to express herself, her body reacted. Her throat began to close up and after quite a while she went to the doctor and was told that there was a growth on her thyroid. Her fifth chakra had been restricted, because she was not speaking her truth. She had had energetic and emotional problems which stopped the proper flow of life-force energy through her body, affecting her physiology. Then she had an even bigger problem.

Cynthia decided to have surgery to remove the growth and half her thyroid. After the surgery she became aware of the power of the fifth chakra and has worked with that energy and consciousness since that time to balance her voice and her behavioral patterns. It has been fifteen years since this occurred in her life and she has not, as of yet, had to take any medication due to an imbalance in hormone production in the thyroid. She learned after that experience to speak her truth — to herself and to others.

The sixth chakra is located in the forehead region of the body. The color is indigo. The sixth chakra governs the physiology of the pituitary gland, the eyes, upper sinus tract and all other body parts in that region of the head. The sixth chakra has several other commonly known names such as the third eye, the mind's eye, the centers of Christ or Cosmic Consciousness.

Within the sixth chakra, both the intuitive center and the intellect are governed. Personally, I love the energy and consciousness of the sixth chakra. It is where I spend most of my time and focus. Moreover, the sixth chakra is the place from which I do my intuitive work. It is home to me. It is the place of empty wisdom, whereby I can hold a neutral center of attention and intention to go in and accomplish the medical intuitive discerning and healing work that I do. It is the safest place from which to do this type of work, due to the fact that it is a place where these energies of neutrality and empty, nonattached wisdom exist.

By focusing your attention in the place of the sixth chakra you can get into and out of other people's energy more safely and do the corrective measures that are required. By working from here you have a greater chance of not becoming emotionally attached to the emotionally-based thought forms that are potential causes of another's disorder or disease. This is important due to the fact that as one steps into another's energy field to do intuitive work it is essential that the intuitive/healing facilitator is in a balanced and unbiased state of awareness. That can happen when you work from the sixth chakra.

You do not lose the compassion for the other person with whom you are working. Your heart center does not close down in any manner of speaking. However, you will have less risk regarding matching emotional pictures with the other person when you place your intuitive focus at your sixth chakra and see, hear, feel and know from there.

Interestingly enough, the cyst I had removed was directly aligned with the point at which the back of the sixth chakra extends from the head. The back of the sixth chakra controls the will of that center — how, when and where to use sixth chakra energy and consciousness. When I had that cyst removed, that process set off the chain of events that led to my illness, to my surgery, to my blindness and to this marvelous regaining of inner intuitive sight. Be not afraid, however, as there are other ways to open up your intuitive center other than brain surgery! The sixth chakra is a wonderful source of energetic ecstasy, of extrasensory perception and of clairvoyance that is available to everyone.

The seventh chakra is located at the crown of the head, and is often symbolized as the thousand-petal lotus. The color is violet purple. Many of you have heard the chants OM, AUM or AMEN, the universal sounds of God which come from and resonates with the seventh chakra. The consciousness that is directed by the seventh chakra is that of your connection to and awareness of the divine within you and the larger divine universal energy, God, in all its wonderful forms and manifestations.

The physiology of the body that is governed by the seventh chakra is the pineal gland. Unfortunately medical science does not know much about the function of the pineal gland. Yet, in some ancient texts it is suggested that the pineal gland is the seat of the soul. A rather fun phenomena that one can experience in the seventh chakra is that wonderful tingling sensation at the crown of the head. One student called that sensation, "Feeling bees at the top of her head." That sensation is a common energetic phenomenon, especially when you are engaged in spiritually-based practice. You can feel these tale-tell sensations at the top of the head when you are deeply enveloped in prayer or meditation. It is a signal that all is well and that you are connected to God's omniscience.

Maybe, if you are just beginning to understand the concepts of chakras, energy and energy medicine, you can think back to times in which you felt this bee-like buzzing at the top of your head. What you were feeling is the energetic activity moving in and around your seventh chakra. Something or someone may have been trying to communicate some information to you energetically. My suggestion is that next time this happens to you, be still and pay attention to any internal guidance or intuitive thoughts you get. Remember, commit to your wisdom.

Connecting with the power and consciousness of the seventh chakra can lead you to pure rapture, unity and bliss. You will feel the purity of your being, for there is no subjective or objective reality as you are truly one with the Father/Mother God.

4

The Power and Use
of Intuition

Some people say that I have a gift — a gift of vision and intuition. I believe that my natural intuitive abilities, which I have experienced to varying degrees since childhood, were brought to the forefront of my awareness by my near-death experience. From that experience the presentation of my intuitive and inner seeing abilities took on the qualities of a gift — something that was suddenly and surprisingly given. However, I know that intuition is a natural part of our humanness.

Intuition is insight that comes to you without utilizing your mental qualities of reasoning or analysis. Intuition is powerful, but not necessarily in the Western sense of the word, which often means power over something or someone.

Intuition is a power that is universally connected to God, to the planet, other people and to the consciousness of all things. By utilizing your intuitive abilities you tap into the mind-stream of innate universal wisdom, which opens up the dimension of the non-local mind. A non-local mind is a mind that is connected to all moments in time, as well as to all people and all places. A non-local mind knows no physical boundaries — it can go anywhere and explore any dimension, as it is one with all things within time and space. Essentially, that is what can be achieved with the practice and honing of your intuitive skills. This oneness, this non-local mind, is what the great Eastern Religions refer to as obtaining enlightenment. It's the same concept, just in different words.

The power and use of your intuitive abilities will allow you to expand your consciousness, your knowingness, inner seeing and/or hearing abilities, as well as your intuitive feeling nature to their ultimate levels. As you work with the exercises in this book your intuition will blossom and unfold into new levels of awareness. You can obtain this heightened state of being. I also refer to this as 360 degree vision. For it is as if nothing past, present or future is veiled from you, no matter where you are or on what you choose to focus.

A key component regarding intuitive development is to know where your integrity lies. With this skill honed you can either help or hurt others, which will affect your life through the process of cause and affect, or karma. Therefore, your intention and attention regarding the development and use of your intuitive facilities must be thought through very seriously. It is incredibly joyful to be able to assist others by intuitive energetic means, yet, quite honestly, you will be challenged to find balance for yourself.

Developing your intuition will most assuredly stretch your consciousness. It has to. Therefore, changes will occur in your life as you proceed. There will be changes that will impact your pathway through life, unfurling your spirit's destiny for you to experience. These changes will ultimately be for your highest good. At times, however, you will find yourself within specific moments that will put you at a crossroads. Your choice(s) regarding whether or not you let go of people, places and events that have been a part of your world may, possibly, not be so easy to deal with. If spiritual growth were easy, we'd all be balls of light right now, not struggling or suffering. Nonetheless, as you proceed with the necessary changes and flow with your newly obtained levels of consciousness you will succeed. No, it may not always be so pleasant. Yet, know that if you are true to your path and stay with it, following your inner truth you will find much joy. Those times of choice, which are seemingly large and challenging, will diminish dramatically as you become clearer and clearer about your spiritually-based intentions.

You must know that as you open each of your intuitive gates, more and more awareness will come upon you. As a result of this, more and more people will seek your assistance. Balance is key. The use of your intuitive wisdom for self-care and wellness is instrumental in regard to maintaining balance within yourself as you grow intuitively. Once more, your integrity is very important. It will be the benchmark and set the stage for a life of joy or one of intuitive stress. You need to ask yourself why you wish to develop your intuitive abilities and to what degree. Is for your own personal gain? Or is it for the betterment of not only yourself, but to lead others to greater awareness as well? The first is a path laden with responsibility that may turn into dissatisfaction, a sense of burden and suffering. The second path is one in which the responsibility is never burdensome and the path is filled with rich rewards on all levels — it is a path of service.

Take a moment and look deep inside so that you can understand, as fully as you can, why you want to develop this part of your natural state of being. It is an important question to ask, from which other important value-based questions will arise. It is an individual choice. Choose wisely as your karma and destiny await.

Two Sacred Laws

In order for your intuitive awareness to strengthen and grow it is imperative that you follow the Two Sacred Laws of Intuitive Development. Sacred Law Number One is to commit to your wisdom. In short, honor and trust your intuitive guidance when it comes to you and do not put it aside. In the process of learning to commit to your inner intuitive wisdom, you will, as you probably already have from time to time, not trust in yourself. Now is the time to start. Take out a piece of paper and write down that you will follow Sacred Law

Number One. You will commit to your intuitive wisdom, honoring and trusting that which comes to you.

Sacred Law Number Two is: live in the moment. All you have, all I have, is this moment and then it is gone, only to be replaced by yet another moment. Live this moment as fully as you can. Do not place worry or burden within your precious moments; that is a distraction and depletion of your energy. There is a Buddhist philosophy that in an abbreviated Western form states: If you cannot do something about an issue — don't worry. If you can do something about an issue — don't worry. It is a condensed version, but accurate nonetheless.

The magic of your intuition will appear as if it is manifesting and developing strength right before your eyes. It will change your life, especially if you combine these two sacred laws and apply them to your life and way of being. When you commit to your intuitive wisdom and trust it in the moment, you will find peace within yourself because you will be more confident in your ability to make correct discernments and choices. As you reach deep inside yourself for your truth, within the context of each moment, and act upon it, your life will progress in a more sacred, intuitive and prosperous manner. After all, your life is demonstrating your truths and beliefs now anyway. So if you are not happy with the way in which you life is going, start trusting that deeper intuitive truth that is within you. Commit to your wisdom, instead of a truth that has been manufactured for you by both your immediate (family-based) and extended (socially-based) cultures.

Does that mean life will be perfect and all will cease to be a struggle or challenge? No. It simply means that by trusting your intuitive wisdom, in the moment, you are living your truth as closely as you can. There will always be learning, as that is the nature of life as a human being — we are here to grow and evolve. However, the learning will be filled with more truth, wisdom and joy than you could possibly imagine. Life will become smoother as well, and this is what makes it so much fun to develop yourself intuitively. Challenges, when they happen, will seem to roll off your back much more easily. You will hold your power in alignment with your wisdom which is connected to God. Fear diminishes, and at times evaporates, when you do this. Trust yourself. Commit to your wisdom in the moment and the evidence of your intuitive accuracy and ability will begin to soar, and so will you. By using these exercises, and combining them with others that you may know of, your intuitive abilities will grow. What will unfold out of your experiences will be the realization that you have the ability to solve any issue(s) in your own life. You may even chose to do what I do, assist people.

A powerful point regarding intuition is that the development of it can connect you more closely to all things. Intuition expands your awareness and places you within the womb of co-creation with God, the planet, all living things and the multitude of dimensions that are elusive to our five-sense way of being. The power of your intuition will open you to the multidimensional nature of the universe. It takes you beyond what is probable in your life to what is possible. Then, as you practice and hone your abilities, you move beyond the world of possibilities and into the realm of potentiality. It is there that the non-local mind and a fully expanded intuitive sense exists — a world in which there is no past, present or future, as there is only one moment in time and space. This moment is a place where everything is knowable and touchable with your intuitive senses. It is a place where the God Force energy inside of you is honored, where you are at peace knowing, in a deep bodily way, that you are one with the universe and all that is.

The Flavors of Intuition

This power and connection to all things that I speak of comes in many different flavors. It allows universal information to flow from the larger primary source into the smaller closed reality. Some of these avenues through which intuitive information can come to you can shock or startle, while others can be subtle and sublimely beautiful, but all are aspects of the same power. The following stories illustrate some of the many different uses and aspects of the power of intuition.

Often, intuition simply taps you on the shoulder and offers a helpful tip or warning. I had just moved to a new area and was just getting home from running some errands. Two young boys were playing in a nearby parking lot beside a series of garages. They were shadowed by the setting sun falling behind the garages making it difficult for them to been seen. I received a strong intuitive hit that they needed to move in case someone came around the corner too quickly. I was intuitively directed and, therefore, understood that if this occurred the driver would not be able to see them in time.

I knew deep inside myself that someone was going to get hurt. It was beyond the logical mind saying that where they were playing was not safe. I knew there was going to be trouble. I hesitated for just a second or two, fearful that they might think I was just some crazy lady. But I quickly thought of my own son and how I would feel if something happened to him. After all, we need to watch out for one another here. I walked over to the boys and asked them to move to another area and told them why. They smiled at me and joyfully ran across the parking lot to an out of the way place. Within 45 seconds of my telling them to move, a young man came speeding around the corner of the garage, driving right through the area where the boys had been playing. The law of cause and effect would have become manifest and someone would have been badly hurt. In this instance, intuition appeared as a little nudge, one of its most common forms. This small "push" probably saved some suffering, and it only took a little trust and commitment to act on it.

Always listen to, trust and act upon your intuitive insights...

Dreams are a strong source of intuitive information and often provide a clearer and more direct connection with your source of truth, especially since your active mind is resting and out of the way. At times dreams may bring important symbols or even whole scenarios concerning events in our future or affecting those we love. Dreams can even allow you to intuitively discern your health and well-being.

A very close friend, Mary, had a strong dream that demonstrates the role that intuition can play in this way. One night she had a dream about her daughter and son-in-law who were living in South Africa. In this dream, the two had died and there was some family debate about where they would be buried. At three o'clock in the morning Mary awoke with this horror of a dream in her head hoping that there was no connection between the dream and reality. At six o'clock, only three hours later, she received a phone call informing her that her son-in-law and daughter had actually been in a head-on auto accident and her daughter came so close to death that she had an out-of-body experience. While this dream didn't provide information on what Mary could do with her life or help her find a lost item, it clearly demonstrated the transpersonal emotional fabric that interconnects us all and is accessible by intuition.

To suddenly realize that intuition is deeply embedded within your life's fabric and to see the implications of how you can be in touch with your source is possibly one of the most beautiful and satisfying emergences regarding the power of your intuition...

Susan, a student and private client, shared an important experience that occurred for her while she was participating in an Intuitive Therapeutics class. During that class, students were guided through the process of doing an intuitively-based chakra and auric field reading on one another. The task was simply to report to their partner the information they received as they intuitively merged with and scanned their classmate's energy. Susan found that as she scanned her partner's body, she saw bright red and yellow flashes of light in and around both of her partner's knees. As well, in the upper part of her partner's body she saw very dark blue energy embedded in the woman's shoulder which ultimately ran down her left arm. After reporting what she was seeing, her partner validated the fact that she had chronic knee pain and that she had just contacted a chiropractor concerning shoulder and arm pain.

Confirmation of this variety happens every day for students and may even seem rather mundane. It is, however, the occasional deep awakening during such an affirmation that best expresses the most powerful and central component of intuition — the primal and beautiful truth of the intimate connection between the largest levels of the universe and self. It was Susan's sheer amazement, the dawning of childlike wonder within her at the immensity of the implications that shocked and thrilled her so — she could intuitively see!

This simple story illustrates the beauty of a person's intuitive trust level expanding. It is a magnificent fact of life that everyone can do this type of work, to varying degrees, depending on their intention and desire to open, grow and soar above mediocrity. Once you have opened up to the larger potential that intuition points to, you might find that your intuition can come with a particular kind of resonance when specific events are going on around you. Or, your intuition may come forth followed by a string of events that seem to carry meaning. It may seem as if symbols, objects and events are put in your path just so you can find them, allowing them to guide you in a new direction or toward a new understanding. An underlying order starts to emerge which suggests an intelligence or power greater than your own that is actively helping you understand your role(s) in the larger picture.

A client and student named Linda found herself surrounded by references to the state of Colorado. It seemed that every time she turned around she would see a Colorado license plate, meet someone from Colorado or pick up a magazine that had a story about Colorado. It quickly became apparent to Linda that the state of Colorado was a place that was calling her, almost demanding that she pay attention to new possibilities that somehow revolved around that area. Linda was trained to listen to her intuition, and took notice and actively started researching Colorado to see what else would resonate for her. As she moved along, she found that more and more events led her to new and important discoveries. She now resides in Colorado with her family. She paid attention to her intuitive wisdom as it came to her in little snippets of information. Then, pulling these pieces together, she found adventure and peace of mind in an environment that serves her.

Intuition delivered by the above means, or by any other delivery mode, will appear as if a new pathway is being set out before you. Simply keep an "eye" open to find each step. With practiced attention, the mysteries of life and your intuitive abilities will unfold before you in a meaningful and productive way.

Accessing Your Intuitive Learning Preference

Developing your intuition takes intention and attention, but it also takes knowing how you uniquely access this type of information, and information in general. Based on years of experience teaching intuitive development, I have found that perhaps the most critical element is understanding how you naturally process information so that you can look in the right places for the doorway to your intuition. Without this element, many people will find their intuitive growth stunted and their information distorted and weak.

Given the fact that all things in the universe are made from energy, the question now is this: how can we begin to sense it? You begin by understanding that you receive your intuitive information, which is a form of energetic stimuli, based on your intuitive learning preference. Your intuitive learning preference is the way in which you access intuitive information most easily. It is the way you prefer to assimilate the external and internal stimuli transferring it into your cognitive thoughts, which can then be articulated and acted upon. Simply put, it is the way you prefer to learn. You may be visual, auditory, empathic or olfactory in nature. Moreover, when it comes to intuitive development you can also be what I call a perceptive learner. Being a perceptive learner means that you have a deep sense of inner knowing. Perceivers may not *see, hear, feel* or *smell* energy in as much as they *know* energy and information is coming to them.

A student, Sheri, once told me that the way she knows intuitive information is coming in for her is that her thoughts seemingly come into her awareness from the side of her body, while her logical thoughts come to her mentally straight on. In short, she knew from what direction her intuitive insights came. For her that was her personalized signal to pay even more attention. Remember, intuition is thought that comes to you without reasoning or analysis, and we all have a personalized way of receiving it. It simply may take a bit of time and practice to discern the way in which you access your intuitive information — but your wellness and life's joy are well worth the effort.

For you to better understand the qualities of your intuitive learning preference, answer the following short questionnaire. It may give you a subtle glance into this part of yourself. If you already know or have a good idea what your cognitive learning preference is — visual, auditory, empathic (sometimes referred to as kinesthetic), olfactory or perceptive — go ahead and answer the questionnaire anyway. You will either be validated for the information you already hold or you may be surprised that something new might come to the surface. Your intuitive learning preference will, more than likely, mirror your cognitive learning preference.

As you proceed with the questionnaire, I would like to say just a word about being an empathic intuitive learner. I want to address this particular intuitive learning preference because it is probably the most misunderstood, yet, is very common. Empathic people access their intuitive information through their body. This sometimes makes it difficult for empathically-oriented people to be in crowded noisy places due to the large volume of potential energetic impacts. Moreover, empathic people's bodies usually have either body weight fluctuations, or hold on to weight, if they continually place themselves in stressful situations. Their bodies automatically layer on adipose tissues, fat, in order to protect themselves emotionally along with certain vital organs. For example: if you are empathic and have been overworking and are stressed out, take a look at whether or not you have added a little extra padding to the back of your waistline to protected your adrenal glands, which will be affected by the stress level you hold in your body. Remember, empaths feel everything around them! The good news is that there are ways to understand how not to take on other people's stress and emotions by developing your intuition.

Note: The questions concerning logic are so that you can determine how much time you spend in your logical/conventional mind. There is nothing wrong with this. However, in reference to intuitive development it is better to put this part of yourself on the shelf until you have honed your intuitive skills enough so that you can incorporate the use of the logical/conventional mind at the appropriate time. There is a difference in conventional intelligence and absolute intelligence. Conventional intelligence is used more often, is more mundane and gets in the way of intuition. It is conventional intelligence, *wherein sit your cognitions. Absolute, or ultimate, intelligence is that which rises above the mundane and does not inhibit higher intuitive levels of learning or understanding. It is your absolute intelligence that is connected to the pure mind of God's absolute intelligence. That is the level of intelligence that needs to be developed. The use of intuition and other meditative practices are the doorways through which one can access the absolute.*

Intuitive Learning Preference Questionnaire

Place a check mark beside the answer that fits you most often. Add up the number of check marks at the end of each section. Interpersonal and intrapersonal questions deal respectively with your preferences to be with other people more, or more within yourself. For example, a person with an interpersonal preference refers to somebody who would like to have the gang over to his or her cave for an ongoing party. An intrapersonal person is one who is more comfortable meditating and being in their cave alone most of the time. A balance between the two is a good way to be — allowing time for introspection, as well as time for practical application of what you have gotten from your inner work and sharing it with the world around you.

Logical
____   I quickly and easily compute numbers in my head.
____   I enjoy figuring out abstract relationships between objects and/or situations.

_____ Whether I am in school or not, I am always fascinated with what is happening on the frontiers of science.

_____ I like to find the answers to "What if" questions, and view my world, most often, from this perspective.

_____ My mind searches for structures, patterns, sequences or a logical order to things and to life.

_____ I enjoy watching or reading about new technological discoveries.

_____ I think that there is a rational explanation for almost everything.

_____ It is easy for me to think abstractly.

_____ I can usually find loop holes or flaws in others' sense of reasoning, and enjoy debating such findings.

_____ I feel comfortable and settled when things have been organized or analyzed.

_____ **Total number checked for *logical*.**

Visual

_____ With my eyes closed, I can usually see images or pictures within my mind's eye.

_____ I am usually sensitive to colors and patterns of colors.

_____ I prefer looking at books and magazines that are mostly filled with illustrations.

_____ I like to keep a visual record of my life and pictures of people, places and events surround me and fill my home and/or office.

_____ I can alter my inner visual perspective and use my imagination to see what something would look like at both microscopic levels and its natural physical size.

_____ I dream in color.

_____ I often have lucid dreams.

_____ I have a good sense of direction by utilizing landmarks.

_____ When I describe something to someone, I can see it easily within my mind's eye.

_____ The worst possible thing that could happen to me would be to lose my eyesight.

_____ **Total number checked for** *visual.*

Auditory

_____ I often have a tune running through my head throughout the day.

_____ I have a pleasant singing voice (and I'm not afraid to use it in the shower!)

_____ When I hear someone else humming a tune I pick it up easily.

_____ I prefer listing to the radio, cassette tapes or CD's instead of watching TV.

_____ I pick up the unique sounds in dialects or accents of people from around the country or world easily.

_____ I remember things better when I hear them being explained to me.

_____ I can often hear noises before other people around me do.

_____ I like to listen to the radio or the television when doing other tasks.

_____ Silence usually drives me crazy.

_____ I often hear voices in my head, instructing me to do this or that. (In reference to intuitive development, it's OK to admit this one!)

_____ **Total number checked for** *auditory.*

Empathic

_____ I love to move my body and I regularly participate in physical activities such as yoga, aerobics, dance or other activities and sports.

_____ I dislike having to sit still for long periods of time.

_____ I feel the energy in a room or environment shortly after I enter into it.

_____ I frequently get insights or ideas when I am involved in physical activity.

_____ I enjoy spending as much time as possible in nature.

_____ I use gestures and other nonverbal actions when I'm engaged in conversations.

_____ I learn things more easily when I can put my hands on them.

_____ I like to do, or have done, daredevil activities like parachuting, bungee jumping, etc.

_____ My body seems to bloat or gain weight when I'm stressed or worried, without necessarily altering my eating habits.

_____ To really learn something, I have to practice it rather
      than read about it or see it on a video or in person.
_____ **Total number checked for** *empathic.*

Olfactory

_____ I can often smell sickness(es) in other people, even
      before they become ill.
_____ I like to sleep with the windows open.
_____ I can often detect odors in my dreams.
_____ In my mind, I can conjure up the smell(s) from past
      events in my life.
_____ I often smell the scent of roses or other fragrances
      when no flowers are present.
_____ When I get upset, I get sinus headaches or congested.
_____ Stuffy rooms make me nervous or uncomfortable.
_____ I can pick out spices used in cooking, just by smelling
      the mixture.
_____ I am very sensitive to fragrances or airborne
      particulates.
_____ I can often smell odors in a space when other people
      cannot.
_____ **Total number checked for** *olfactory.*

Interpersonal

_____ People seek me out for advice or counsel.
_____ I would rather participate in team sports than individual
      ones.

_____ When I have problems I prefer to seek help from other people rather than having to work them out alone.

_____ I have at least three close friends.

_____ I enjoy playing social games like Monopoly, Bridge and/or Poker instead of games like Solitaire or computer games.

_____ I don't need much alone or quiet time.

_____ When I see something that needs doing, I do it.

_____ I have been called a leader, and I consider myself one.

_____ I am involved in my local school, neighborhood, church or community in some way.

_____ I would rather spend Saturday night at a get-together, than spend it at home alone.

_____ **Total number checked for *interpersonal*.**

Intrapersonal

_____ I have a regular time to meditate, reflect and/or think about my life.

_____ I have attended classes, seminars and workshops to gain insight about myself and to experience personal growth.

_____ I am somewhat iconoclastic, and my opinions often distinguish me from others.

_____ I prefer hobbies, pastimes or doing activities by myself.

_____ I have specific goals for my life that I think about on a regular basis.

_____ I have a realistic view of my own strengths and weaknesses.

_____   I enjoy spending a weekend in a cabin or hideaway.

_____   I am independent and strong willed.

_____   I have a journal or diary to record the events of my
inner life.

_____   I am self-employed, or I have seriously considered
owning my own business.

_____   **Total number checked for** *intrapersonal.*

What did you discover about yourself by answering these questions? The importance of this questionnaire is to bring into your awareness that there are many ways in which you can access intuitive information and energetic stimuli — and to find out what your specific preference is. In so doing, you will discover where your strengths lie when it comes to accessing this type of information.

As well, please understand that you don't have to have just one pathway or learning preference through which your intuition comes to you. Many of us are intuitively wired in multiple ways. For example, in my case I use my *seeing, feeling, hearing* and *knowing* pathways to do the work that I do. Sometimes the pathway I use is dependent on the person I am reading. Sometimes it is the environment that causes me to utilize one skill level over another. So don't get hung up on being one way or another. Just ride along with where you are now and know that you will probably add more learning preference pathways as you practice and develop your intuition.

This potential for change when it comes to accessing intuitive information is what I refer to as "intuitive learning preference duration." Currently, you may be visually oriented; however, six months from now you may make a shift and become more empathic which, again, is the ability to feel people's and environmental energy(ies) more easily. In brief, the length of time during which you utilize this specific intuitive learning preference will most likely change, usually for the better, as your life progresses. This change is most likely due to your increases in your intuitive development and ability, although personality maturation may be a cause as well.

It is helpful to remember that life is full of cycles and nothing really ever stays the same, including your intuitive learning preference. Many things can happen as you stretch and increase your consciousness, and most likely will. Use the questionnaire as a launching pad, applying the concepts of learning preferences to intuitive development. Many students find it helpful, as it gives them permission to be who they are and not have to *see* in order to work intuitively.

Remember, as you develop into the spiritual being that you are — working, laughing, loving, and practicing life's challenges within this physical vessel — give yourself a break now and then. Be gentle with the way in which you move through the world. Be gentle with yourself and the way in which you learn. Search and grow toward your development. Use tools like the awareness of your intuitive learning preference(s) as markers, which will assist you in mapping your intuitive developmental progress and your life's process. Know that one of the single most powerful tools, which will stay a constant in your life, will be your innate wisdom — your intuition.

So many people say that they want to *see* like I do. Generally, I point out that they, too, will be able to access their intuitive information very effectively, once they find their particular way in which it comes to them. It's important for you to discover the specific or combined intuitive learning preference(s) that constitute your clearest channel(s). As you practice the exercises, pay attention. As you move through your daily life, suddenly getting flashes of intuition more regularly, pay attention to the emotional, bodily, and mental sensations that announce, relay and conclude the giving of that intuitive information to you. Moreover, remember the Two Sacred Laws: commit to your wisdom and live in the moment.

An example that illustrates how each of us accesses intuition differently and how often we feel insecure about speaking our intuitive truth took place when I was lecturing at a convention in Tucson, Arizona. After my lecture there was the usual group of warmhearted souls waiting for some personal time with me. I noticed that one woman hung back and was the last one with whom I spoke. She told me that her name was Mary, and that she was a nurse in an intensive care unit at a local hospital. She related to me that she would *smell* the fragrance of flowers around certain patients when they were about to cross over from this life into the next. She further told me of her experiences with smelling foul odors around some patients just prior to them taking a sudden turn for the worse.

Mary touchingly shared how she could sense all these things and could therefore act more appropriately toward her patients, taking care of them with greater concern based on her olfactory intuition.

She was painfully aware that there was no one at work with whom she could dare share her experiences. As Mary continued with her story, her eyes welled up with the emotions regarding her years of secret intuitive work and service to her patients. She knew she had this heightened state of intuitive awareness, but she didn't know where to turn. She had no one to talk with about her intuitive experiences. We paused together in the hallway, shared stories for a few brief moments and then she went on her way. As Mary walked away, I was confident that all of the patients who were touched by this woman had been truly graced and blessed. She was someone who was sensitive to their needs and situation. Mary is the type of nurse I would want attending to my needs.

This illustrates that you don't have to be visually oriented on an intuitive level to access your information clearly. Mary was certainly tuned in to what was most natural for her. It is important to realize that it has been society that has set forth the myth, "I'll believe it when I see it." You, as an intuitive individual, don't have to accept that myth any longer. You can trust your intuitive information based on the way you access it most easily. Besides, that myth is more accurately stated, by cosmic law, the other way around — "believe it and then you'll see it."

Another wonderful example of understanding your learning preference is that of a charming and warm student named Sasha who had worked as a computer analyst. After completing the Level One training program of Intuitive Therapeutics, Sasha timidly began to hang out her healing shingle and is now in the process of continuing her intuitive training in order to be her best at this new career. Sasha *hears* the chakras through the various tones as they resonate. By receiving her intuitive information in the way she accesses it best, she can detect imbalances within a person's system by literally hearing the sour tones within their body. Therefore, she knows where to adjust their energy. As it is with Sasha, other intuitives and yourself, committing to your intuitive wisdom allows you to make more accurate assessments and facilitate a client's education and healing.

I have found through my travels and sharing that many of you have had the same experiences I have had. We have all been receiving intuitive information our entire lives. The unfortunate thing is that most are afraid to share it. Please don't be afraid anymore. Be discerning certainly, but trust and own your intuitive wisdom. It is so very important. Own who you are. Not trusting and owning this wondrous component clogs your energetic system. This can cause dissonance, misalignment and possibly even disease within you. Always speak your intuitive truth, to yourself and others. It is about honoring a wonderful innate part of who you are as a component of the whole.

I'll never forget the look on one woman's face in class when she finally understood that it was OK for her just to *know* what was going on in reference to her intuitive guidance. For years Karen thought she was wrong because she didn't see pictures or hear voices in her head. She just knew. She is a perceiver — yet for all those years she didn't trust herself or commit to her wisdom. She was very relieved and grateful for a new way of looking at the ability she knew she had, yet, hadn't given herself permission to use. Karen's intuitive development thereafter was swift.

These few simple stories illustrate that we all have a different pathway through which we harvest the vast amounts of divine intuitive information available. By honoring the way in which intuitive wisdom can be most easily gathered and acted upon, we create a better quality of life and wellness for ourselves and for everyone around us.

By now I hope you understand and can feel deeply within your body that your intuitive information has always been an innate part of you, even if it has been hidden or ignored. More importantly, you can now trust its existence and trust the way in which your intuitive wisdom comes to you. You simply need to find your source and the conduit through which it passes. Keeping in mind that yours may be different from everyone else's — please honor that. Everyone is different and everyone moves at his or her own pace.

Developing Your Intuitive Awareness, Mindfully

Now that you recognize that you are intuitive and have discovered your intuitive learning preference, it is time to understand what may transpire as you begin to step into and develop the depth and breadth of your intuition. Remember that life is a process and not an event. That statement can be appropriately applied towards intuitive development also. There most assuredly will be events as you progress; nonetheless, for the most part it is a process. So don't wait for those lightning bolts of instant illumination. It will happen as you move through the veils that have hidden this innate part of yourself.

Intuitive development is wrapped in the essence of mindfulness. Being mindful is the practice of becoming awakened to the vast stimuli that surround all things without attachment. The essence of mindfulness comes from deep within the belly of Buddhism. To be mindful is to behave in a manner in which one is awake and aware of the subtleties around them and therefore capable of responding to them instead of reacting.

Currently, we use only a small percentage of our brain's capacity. Therefore, one could assume we are living and moving through our lives being aware of a small amount of what is truly happening around us. In other words, if, as you draw open the curtains to the window of your world, you only open them to just a fraction of their capability, you allow only a directly proportional amount of illumination into your mind.

Mindfulness will open the doors of your soul and mind through which intuition will walk. It has been my experience that the cultivation of intuition and mindfulness go hand in hand. They are opposite sides of the same coin, if you will. They always show up together and it is vital that you develop your intuitive perspective in a mindful manner. Pay attention. Be awake. As you cultivate mindfulness, your intuition will grow — it cannot help but do so. As your intuition develops and builds, you become more mindful of your environment. For these two components are part of an infinite universal cycle. You cannot have one without the other. They are mechanisms interwoven within the system of natural protocols, which lead to the development of consciousness. As you develop your intuitive abilities you will gain a greater understanding of the interconnectedness between all things and their systems of cycles. You will shed the limited perspective of consciousness that deals with duality and a three dimensional perspective as the only true, hard reality. Your time and process undertaken in the development of intuition will guide you to the absolute (ab-soul-ute) and ultimate way of being

Your Progress Is Equal to Your Practice

Your progress is going to be equal to your practice. There is simply no substitute for a well thought out and motivated practice. What a practice is and how it is developed is discussed below and exercises throughout the book should be used per instructions. The easiest way to talk about what a practice is, is to discuss what aspects are embodied within a daily practice and the definition of a practice will emerge for you.

First, your daily practice involves the development of discipline. The discipline you cultivate will assist you in creating the space in your life for your practice, and that discipline will transfer into other areas as well. Practice is about the personal honor and loyalty that you show to yourself and to your chosen path. Your daily practice is formed by a particular level of devotion — devotion to your spirit/body/mind and to your spiritual source (God, Christ, Buddha, Great Spirit, Allah, Universal Light, Intelligence, Pure Mind or Source).

Beyond the development of discipline, the sharing and experiences of life have within it many striations of learning processes. These are filled with synchronicities, lightning bolts of illumination, dark nights of the soul, wondrous events, subtle practices and experiences — all of which support and build upon one another assisting in your growth. It is a complex system that matches your own internal intricacies — the macro supporting the micro.

Within your practice, natural protocols which lead to greater depth of understanding and inner wisdom will emerge and develop. You will call upon these every day in both a formal and informal manner. These protocols are a spiritual formula and are a way of taking care of yourself. The components to your spiritual formula may consist of, but are not limited to, such things as prayer, meditation, physical exercise, visualization exercises, proper nutrition and the development of proper speech toward yourself and others. Again, the exercises in this book are designed to assist you in developing your daily practice. It is up to you to decide the protocols you will follow and exactly what you want to be a part of your spiritual formula.

Your daily practice becomes a lifetime commitment of cultivating your soul-self, which desires so deeply to blossom within you. It is my prayer that you can grasp the broader picture involved when I speak of the importance of developing your intuition. Intuition is a cornerstone upon which your practice rests. Like your daily practice, your intuition is developed through the art of applying what you mindfully *hear, feel, see* or *know* to daily events within your life.

It really is quite simple. We all know that to become accomplished at anything you have to practice the skills required for reaching your goal. If you want to be a healthy, conscious and well-balanced soul within a physical body, living your definition of heaven on earth, you develop your intuition and a daily spiritual practice mindfully. You could say that your intuition is a reflection of the development of your soul's internally grown and externally exemplified way of being. Try to objectively look at your present level of intuitive development and see within it the reflected openness and connectedness to your soul-self, or lack thereof. No matter what you *see, feel, hear* or *know* about yourself and your current state of development, you can always improve upon it. You do so by developing your daily practice and tapping into the eternal well of innate soul wisdom.

In order for you to develop intuitively, you need to take some preliminary steps down your path. These steps lead to the development of your protocols and spiritual formula. First and foremost it is essential that you make a commitment to yourself and your growth — no matter what may cross your path or whatever might try to stop that growth. Secondly, and you have already done this, you need to identify your current intuitive learning preference. Thirdly, you need to become more aware of your own energy and the way in which you utilize it. This is a process that happens naturally once you make the commitment. As you step forward in these ways, you will be responsible for attempting to awaken your sleeping consciousness — this is done, in part, through practicing the exercises included in this book that speak to your soul.

This particular study of intuitive development is based on the threefold Intuitive Therapeutic model. It consists of three main ingredients — consciously moving energy through your body; meditation, prayer and/or concentration; and physical movements. All three must be done at some point in time everyday. However, don't be concerned if you have a busy life and don't know where it will fit. Your discipline, devotion and commitment will find the time for you.

5

Disciplines That Develop
and Nourish Intuition

You are intuitively told everything you need to know
all of the time...
Are you listening to the whispers?

(If you haven't already done so, begin a journal so you can record your experience. Additionally, please read through the entire exercise prior to engaging in it. There are usually a series of steps within each one that needs to be understood prior to doing the exercise.)

When doing any of these exercises, know that you are always in control. Where you hold your intention and attention will bring about the results of your focus. It is that way with your life and your spiritual practice as well as with the visualizations you will be doing within this context. These exercises have been used in my daily practice, and with clients and workshops for years. Thousands of people have used them and have brought them into their daily life. These disciplines work. They open up your intuition.

When your intuition is opened you are able to discern more easily what you can and want to do with your life and life-force energy. In addition, you will be in receivership of more and more intuitive insights. As you begin to recognize these intuitive hits, your belief in your intuitive self strengthens. As your belief strengthens, you naturally begin to trust your own process and wisdom. It is then that true commitment to your inner power will take place, which empowers you to mindfully move in a more centered way through your environment. Commit to your wisdom and trust your intuition as it unfolds through these exercises. Rest assured that your intuitive wellness will come forth as well.

Creating Sacred Space

I was facilitating an evening meditation gathering when one of the attendees asked me a question regarding the lack of vitality she was experiencing. We discussed several things, one of which was a question I posed to her. I ask her what was in the Northeast portion of her home. "My living room couch, which I frequent quite often," she responded. I asked about this section of her home because I was picking up on an overwhelming sensation of stagnant energies which both demonstrated and reflected her body's energy(ies). It was obvious that it didn't matter whether she was home or not. Her home's space, particularly the couch area, mirrored and held the energies of a more important and intimate space — her body. How could she gain, and more importantly maintain, vitality when she would come home after hours of exercise and plop on a couch that held stagnant energy?

The couch and surrounding energies were denser and slower than her body's energy. When she exercised, she would regain some vitality through that process and therefore, her body's energetic density would be more highly charged. This occurred as a result of the more pronounced breathing, allowing more life-force energy into her body, as well as the naturally occurring biochemical releases which occur doing exercise. It is interesting to note that while she had created a new and sacred space within her body through refinements in diet and exercise, she had forgotten to create a sacred space in which her body is held — her home. To do so would assist her in sustaining more vitality and vital energies throughout — emotionally, physically, spiritually and energetically.

The more you progress on your spiritual path, the more you desire closeness to those higher levels of conscious-ness — to embody God in his or her many forms. You engage in your spiritual dance, doing practices that will awaken that which already resides within you. As you bring God into your consciousness, you should naturally create room within your home environment for that energy/consciousness as well. After all, you bring food into your house before you bring it into your physical body — your most intimate house.

The environment in which you live, work, meditate, visualize, play and pray performs an important role regarding the efficacy of your practice and your overall wellness. As you develop your mindfulness and intuitive abilities, you will be able to stay calm and centered within the most raucous situations and environments. To get to that place inside of you, it is always wise to have a sacred space within your own home in which to practice. Creating this type of space in your home and in your life demonstrates and reflects the level of calmness and centeredness you hold within your being — as within, so without.

Your sacred space does not have to consist of an entire room or wing of your home — it can be on a tabletop in your favorite room. Creating sacred space within your bedroom is always nice because as you enter the sleep and dream state at night you have a wonderful energy of consciousness already set in place, surrounding you. Your consciousness is highly suggestible when you are in the sleep state, so why not be the one who sets the space that your consciousness rests within?

If you are really crowded for space, or the person(s) with whom you living doesn't understand or resonate with your spiritual quest, you don't have to put your spirituality on display. The creation of a sacred space is for you. What truly matters is what resides within your heart space, although, having a sacred space within your home can lift you out of the occasional shadowed corner of the human experience — and assist you through the periodic darkened night of the soul.

Being limited by living space allows you to create a portable alter. Simply take a smaller piece of cloth, a 12x12 piece works wonderfully well, and keep your sacred items on top of it. When you are not engaged within a practice of some kind, simply wrap up your items and store them in the cloth. Place the bundle in a dresser drawer or a box when not in use. When you are ready to meditate, pray or do whatever practice you use to enhance your spiritual growth, place your altar items reverently on the cloth before you begin. When you are finished, thank and bless the items for their assistance, gently wrap them back up in the cloth and put them away.

Now what can you put on your altar? A good foundation is always important, so it is nice to have a decorative piece of fabric or cloth upon which to set your items. It is preferable to select something that is made of a natural or even organic fabric such as wool, cotton or silk. These are easily available and come in a wide variety of colors and patterns. Items that you set upon your altar should have significant meaning for you. They need to touch your soul. You might want to have a bouquet of fresh flowers or a single flower bud if space is a consideration. Items such as rocks, crystals, fossils or feathers that you have found or purchased from an interesting place add grounded earthy energy.

You can place any size picture of a loved one or of an exalted master that touches you on your altar. Pictures of masters such as Christ, Mary, Buddha, Hindu Gods or Goddesses, a cherished Guru, or pictures of indigenous guides and symbols are all appropriate. After all, this is your sacred

space and your altar should bring into it those energies and
levels of consciousness that are meaningful to you.
Furthermore, having such masters present will assist you in
keeping focused on whatever level of consciousness you
would like to resonate with and therefore achieve.

It is also important to know that your sacred space,
whether it is contained within a drawer, sits upon a tabletop or
is spread throughout your living space, will most likely change
as you change. As your spirit grows and soars, the
demonstration of how you express your spirit and spirituality
will change accordingly. All things are impermanent. Think of
the beautiful and meaningful sand paintings of the Native
Americans, or of the colorful sand mandalas of the Tibetan
Buddhists. They are sacred spaces filled with holy artistic
meanings, created to evoke energies and certain levels of
consciousness for particular events. They are beautiful and
used for worship within their cultural context, then destroyed,
displaying non-attachment to form — releasing the spirit.

Introduction to Your Soul — A Visualization

This visualization will introduce you to someone
whom you may not have seen or connected with in a long
time, if ever. It will connect you with your soul — the
consciousness and energy that is your connection to God and
all that is. This is a very simple exercise that is quick and easy to
do. After you engage in this exercise, you may wonder why it
has taken so long to view this wondrous part of yourself!

The directions are simple. It is always best to have a peaceful space. If you have gathered materials for your altar already, invoke that sacred space and allow it to enfold you. You may choose to play some soft, soothing music in the background. Next, sit comfortably, upright in a chair, gather your thoughts inward and let go of the outside world. Now ask that an image of your soul be presented to you. *See, feel, hear* or *know* that something will materialize in your mind's eye and/or feeling nature. You may see an image that looks similar to a human form. Or you may see sparks of light or larger balls of light. Set the intention and hold your attention clearly so that you can be introduced to your own magnificence.

Sit quietly while the image(s) appear(s). Commit to your intuitive wisdom and don't sweep away any images in disbelief. *Listen to, see, feel* and *know* your spiritual truth and knowledge — trust what comes before you. You are asking to see who you are — your true self — which is an awesome gift and experience.

Once you have the image in front of you, ask any question you desire. If you have been struggling with a particular problem, now is the time to ask for assistance. Listen and take in any information that may be given to you. When you are finished receiving these insights that your soul's image has for you, invite this image to join you within your physical body. This is accomplished by *seeing, feeling* or *knowing* that this energetic mind's-eye form of your soul is gently and safely merging with your body. If the image is in a human-like or angelic form, watch as this image sits down inside of your body, allowing it to slide into your body like a hand slides into a glove. If the image is a spark or ball of light, or any other image, allow it to merge with your body in the way in which you are directed to do so.

Obviously, if there is any hesitation on your part to invite this soulful energy and consciousness inside of your physical form, trust that knowledge as well. The initial time may not be the time in which you are to merge. I have yet to see any negative demonstration regarding this exercise. After all, you are in charge of your energy and your space. You are invoking your spirit. Nothing will harm you. Simply move at your pace, in accordance with your guidance. Again, you are in control of this. You will not see anything that will be other than your soul's image — for that is your intention.

When you are finished with this exercise, take a few minutes to write down your experience in your journal. If at anytime you are feeling weak, sad or out of control, sit down, quiet your mind and body, and then ask that your soul come to you. Next, ask for the information that you need and merge the energy of your soul with the energy of your physical body. It has been my experience and the experience of others that when you join with that level of energy, wondrous things appear, challenges lessen and peace begins to bathe you.

Creating Energetic and Spirit-based Wholeness – A Visualization

This is a wonderful way to regain your energy, inner strength and focus. In many shamanic traditions it is believed that when traumatic events occur, part of the soul or spirit of that person is lost or fragmented. I'm certain that you can remember times in your life when you have either had the wits scared out of you or been in a severely traumatic encounter.

Many of you are the same as I and have had spiritually induced out-of-body experiences, but there is no spirit loss here. There can be, however, spirit loss in spiritually sought after out-of-body experiences if they are facilitated by someone who is inexperienced or loses track of your energy during the process. Nonetheless, spiritually induced experiences are when a universal force steps in and sweeps you out of your body. Believe me, you are being guided and protected by the absolute, God, and there will be no soul loss — only soulful gain.

Spirit-directed experiences — when God steps in and says, "Hello," — are not what I am referencing here. I am talking about experiences such as the one I had during my brain surgery when I remember being up in the corner of the operating room looking down at the rather interesting things going on there. Things that were not so pleasant to view — my head bolted and screwed to the operating table and part of my skull sitting over in a container of some kind. You know, those types of things. I know this experience separated me, to some degree, on an energetic and spirit-based level. These are the types of out-of-body experiences I am talking about. Ones that are shocking, filled with crises, horror or prolonged suffering of any kind — even verbal or physical abuse. Anything that drains and takes your spirit away from you.

Separation of your energy and spirit from your physical body can happen in subtle ways as well. So many times we feel drained after running hither and yon for the benefit of our families, loved ones, friends or careers. Hardly ever do we feel stretched and exhausted as a result of taking a lot of time for ourselves, as it is usually someone else's energy to which we are tending. It is fine to be in service to others, but there must be balance in all things.

This process will assist you in reestablishing your energetic wholeness, bringing you back to balance. It will help you call your spirit back — the spirit-filled, life-force energy that you have been sending out to others or that has been shocked out of your system. It will help alleviate the feelings that are associated with this type of loss — feeling slightly fatigued, scattered, unfocused and/or so exhausted that you are literally physically ill.

Simply sit or lie down in a quiet space. Create your sacred space around you as you have done before. Draw your attention inward and hold the intention that you are going to summon back to you your spirit and life-force energy that has been either taken from you, given away by you or lost through some mutual exchange. Take a few slow deep breaths, exhaling all of the tension out and away from your body. Ask for any helping guides to assist you. Call in God, Universal Intelligence, The Light, Christ, Holy Mother Mary, Lord Buddha, Lord Shiva, angels, animal spirits and/or those who walk with you in spirit to come and be with you. Call in the supportive force that resonates with you and don't judge that which someone else my call forth for them. (All paths lead to the same door, there are just different knocks.) They will help protect you and the space around you as you call your spirit back.

Now *see, feel* or *know* that you are placing a veil of light and pure consciousness around your physical body. This veil is porous in nature, yet protective. It is like a screen which will only allow the purity of your spirit to penetrate it and settle back into your body. That which does not belong to you will not be able to penetrate through this veil of God consciousness. This statement is part of your intention. This veil can appear to you as light, coming in one single or a variety of colors and thicknesses. Let your creative cousins — imagination and intuition — guide you through this process. Remember to commit to your wisdom, let the image(s) come forth and trust.

When you have this veil in place, with a commanding voice, call back your spirit and energy. You may wish to say something like this out loud. "I command all parts of my spirit and fragments of energy to come back from the places and people to whom I have given them. I wish to regain my strength and focus once more." If you believe in past lives you can add that you are "commanding your spirit and energy back from beginningless time onward." You might as well cover all of those lifetime bases, so to speak. (As a side note, many have reported seeing visions of other times and places, outside of their current cultural context, when they call their spirit back from beginningless time onward. Just think of all that you have left behind, year after year, lifetime after lifetime.)

Once you have stated your intention, "to command and reestablish your energy and spirit within your own body," *see, feel* or *know* that it is returning to you. Know that all of the places and people you have connected with are sending it back to you, graciously. Prior to your spirit's energy entering into your physical body, allow it to pass through the veil of pure consciousness around your body. This will allow everything to be cleansed and purified. By doing this, you will not have anyone else's energy in your body. It is yours and yours alone.

In addition, I suggest that you work with energetic mapping here as well. In short, watch or feel the places that the energy, light or colors settle back into within your body. The areas that the energy goes to are indicative of the areas from which your energy had left in the first place. This is highly valuable information. For instance, if you do this exercise repeatedly after work everyday, you may find that your energy comes streaming back into a particular chakra area. If your third chakra is indicated by a stream of energy flowing into it and a picture of your superiors or a particular coworker comes into your mind's eye every time you do this, that is indicative of their energy infiltrating your system in some manner during work. You are losing your energy, spirit, vitality and wellness to them from that chakra. The consciousness that you hold there is being compromised by their level(s) of consciousness. Do you want that to continue?

By doing this exercise you will not only reestablish your spirit within you, but you will be able to identify the primary location(s) from which you either give and/or share your life-force and spirit's energy. From there, you can use other exercises found within this book to rebalance your energetic system, after you have called yourself back home, so to speak.

It is very common that these types of patterns are revealed to those who choose to do this simple exercise. Again, it will show you where within the energetic and physical structures of your body you are losing your spirit's energy. As a result of having this type of information about yourself you will be more aware and centered when around those people or places. Therefore, you will not be so subject to losing this vital life force power.

Running the Rainbow

Running the Rainbow is both a wonderful experience and practice. The mechanics of this exercise first came to me during my near death experience in 1982. If you recall from chapter one of this book, it was when I was standing on the edge of a forest, gazing longingly at the trees as well as at the souls that were walking contemplatively amongst one another that I had this experience. I so wanted to join those souls in the forest, but knew that this was a quiet place, one filled with reverence. Therefore, I chose to merely observe and stay on the outside of the forest, standing on some heavenly grass.

It was while I was standing on this grass that I felt a surge of love-filled energy rise up through my feet as they connected to the earth-like surface. The energy continued to lift up my legs, into the torso of my being, up through my head, fountaining out the top of my head and cascading down my arms and out my hands. The overwhelming sense of gratitude that flooded from my heart merged with this love and literally poured from me back onto the grass upon which I was standing. The result was that not only was I being cleansed and fed, my gratitude and love fed the grass as well. The exchange was powerful! My being felt crystalline and vibrantly alive.

It was years later that I met a woman who shared with me an exercise in which she used the colors of the chakras. My body's memory clicked in and linked the two experiences together, which allowed Running the Rainbow and the process of energy mapping to emerge. I have also heard of and practiced similar exercises, visualizing the colors of the chakras as pools of water that flow through you in a cleansing manner.

It is the process of energetic mapping while utilizing the exercise of Running the Rainbow that makes it an extra-ordinarily powerful experience. When done over time this is an excellent tool which will allow you to become more aware of the way in which energy moves through your body on a broad spectrum level. It will act as a roto-rooter, clearing unwanted energetic debris and influences out of your auric field, and ultimately your physical body.

As well, and this is important, I highly recommend you record your experience each time you do this exercise. By writing down your experience in your journal you will discover the bones, so to speak, of who you are energetically. You will discover the energetic structure by which you create and hold on to the thought forms that sustain your reality. Writing down your experience is necessary to work through what I call "energy mapping." Mapping is the process by which you will discover submerged patterns of energy, emotions, thought forms and behaviors. The process of "energy mapping" happens through writing down your experiences as though you were simply the observer and therefore objectively reporting how the colors move through your body. Over time, as you continue to work with these exercises, patterns and commonalties regarding the way in which your energy flows will begin to emerge. Mapping is the process of charting your experience in order to gain information regarding the most effective way you can begin to utilize your life-force energy. In addition, as you work with this particular exercise over time, say in thirty days if you do it once a day, you will be able to discern much more clearly what serves you in your life and what doesn't.

How does that happen? During the process of Running the Rainbow you are bringing into your body the colors of the rainbow — red, orange, yellow, green, blue, indigo and violet — through your physical and energetic layers that invisibly surround your physical body. We know scientifically that colors have and hold vibrational rates within their molecular structure that are specific to each particular color band. As well, we know that your bones and muscle tissues, as well as your vital organs and all other bodily components, have and hold a specific vibrational rate that is relative to that particular body component.

When you run the colors of the rainbow one by one through your body, the color's vibrational rate will affect your body's vibrational rate — both overall and within each individualized structural section of the body. In addition to affecting your body's vibratory rate, any person's or place's energy that may have temporarily taken up housekeeping somewhere within your body's energetic field will be affected by the color's vibratory rate as it passes through your system(s) causing changes, albeit subtle in the beginning.

Furthermore, it is important for you to understand that this practice will stir your pot. It will reveal things that have been held within your emotional being that may feel a bit uncomfortable for you to look at. There has been no instance in my years of experience of someone finding out more about themselves than they can handle. Looking at the depth and breadth of who you are and where you currently are, as well as being willing to expand yourself even further, is what spiritual work is all about. Rest assured that you would not be reading this book or doing this work if you were not prepared for the adventures that will be brought forth from your soul and into your life. Your life is a precious, awesome gift. By working with this technique you will soon recognize all the wonderment that is within you and therefore the wonderment that you can bring forth into your world.

Running the Rainbow — A Visualization

Starting with an awareness of one's self is not narcissistic. If you are to love others, you must first love yourself. If you are going to be at peace with the environment you have created as your reality, you must first be at peace within your inner reality. In your process of creating and maintaining both a loving and a peaceful balance in your world you must first recognize your connection to that river of life-force energy that flows in and around you. This river moves through you and on to others and encompasses all of the colors of the rainbow. At times, some colors are more prevalent within the electromagnetic field than others and that is often due to your current state of wellness. In other words, how you're feeling about yourself and your world, mentally, physically, emotionally and spiritually. Along with that, the various energies and levels of consciousness that are flowing in and out of your life and your body show up within the electro-magnetic field as colored bands and currents of energy.

By gently incorporating this exercise into your daily life, your intuitive abilities will become more apparent. In addition, as you use this exercise, you will clean out the chakra system of your body and remove blockages that were hindering you. You will move not only consciousness (thought forms) and energy but the emotions within. You will begin to know on a deeper

level that you can trust yourself and commit to your intuitive
wisdom. It is time to recognize that you already know what is
best for you, your body and your energy. The task at hand is to
offer yourself the space within and begin the process.

You begin this exercise by grounding yourself. This is
done simply by using your mind's eye (the sixth chakra) and
imagining cords or roots that extend from the soles (souls) of
your feet, allowing them to sink deeply into the earth, following
them with your mind's eye and seeing how deeply they
penetrate through the earth's crust. Now sit and be with this
grounded feeling, sensing the energy of the earth and your
connection to it. Know that you are safe, secure and cannot
make any errors as you proceed. You are working with your
body's energy — your energy — you cannot make an error.
Even if the cords that extend from your feet go through the
earth and out into space to find a connection to another planet,
that is perfectly fine. That happened for a student of mine. At
first she thought she may not have been doing it right. But she
was. She was being open to the way in which she felt
grounded and connected. She let her intuition and her spirit
guide her process.

Now, visualize the following colors rising up through
the grounding cords or roots. Allow them to flow upward
through your body one at a time. Work with the colors in this
order at first, then trust your intuitive wisdom as to the order
that needs to be applied to this exercise. What follows are the
order and the colors: Red — first chakra; orange — second
chakra; yellow — third chakra; green — fourth chakra; sky
blue — fifth chakra; indigo — sixth chakra; purple — seventh
chakra (all the colors of the rainbow). Again, run each color,

one at a time, up through the grounding cords connected to your feet and up through your body. Allow the color to move all the way up through your body to the top of your head. Allow the color to branch off at the throat and cascade down your arms, running out the palms of your hands.

After you get the mechanics down, what follows next is energy mapping. As you run your rainbow, holding your mind in the place of the observer, examine how the color feels while it's in your body. Is it warm, hot, cool or cold? Notice the texture of the color, of the energy (if there is any), as well as the way in which the color flows through the body and the ease with which each color flows.

Notice if any pictures seemingly pop into your mind as you run a particular color. Does a person or an event that you haven't thought of in years, months or days come to mind? Pay attention to every detail, play with it, relax and trust yourself — just let things happen.

Change from one chakra color to the next by replacing the color with the next color in line. For example, running red, first chakra energy is replaced by bringing orange, second chakra energy. Simply allow the red, or preceding color to continue to flow out the top of your head and the palms of your hands while the new color, in this case orange, begins to flow up through the grounding cords and into the body. Run each color through your body as long as you like; you'll know when it's time to switch colors.

I would suggest that you work with this exercise for at least 30 days in a row. You will see changes if you do. As well, some people find it difficult to run their energy from the feet upward, yet, find it easy to bring the energy and color down from the cosmos, through the head and body then ground it into the earth. It is fine if you choose to do it that way. It simply allows for a different perspective. However, let me say that the reason I suggest you run your rainbow from the ground up is that it will ground you in your body.

Many on the spiritual path find it easy and preferable to be up in the ethers, so to speak, engaging in upper chakra resonance. They find it difficult to bring in the colors andvibrations of the lower chakras. However, that is exactly what you need to be doing. Grounding your energy and spirit within the physical body is why you are here in the first place. We are spirit. We are already very, very good at being spirit, floating and dancing in the ethers. You have chosen this precious earth birth to learn to be here now, solidly.

Releasing Energy from Within

This exercise has two primary functions and benefits. First, it will increase your intuitive awareness because the sixth chakra, the place of intuitive wisdom, is the primary focus of your attention and intention. After all, we know that that which we focus on becomes reality. I would like to place your attention up in the sixth chakra, as if there is a tiny version of yourself, looking out a small window located within your forehead. Hold your attention and focus there as you proceed with this exercise. As a reminder, the sixth chakra will be your constant focus, the place from which you *see, feel, hear* and *know*, while you work with, not only the sixth, but the other chakras and central nadis channels as well. Secondly, this exercise will assist you in the releasing of unwanted energy(ies) from within the chakras and nadis, as well as release unwanted levels of consciousness that are hiding out and taking refuge in your body's energetic system. Remember that the nadis are the pathways through which energy and thought form(s) are transferred from one chakra to another. They are your energetic telephone lines, so to speak.

I am using the sixth chakra in the directions, but you can use any chakra you wish. Know that whichever chakra you focus on you will be heightening your intuitive state of awareness.

To begin, focus your attention in the sixth chakra. Now take your mind's eye and go within your body approximately 1/4 to 1/2 inch inside your forehead. This point will be the ending point of the Sushumna nadi, the central channel. You will know, intuitively, when you have reached the proper place within your body. Trust what you receive. Now, *see, feel, hear* or *know*, a droplet of light emerging from this end point of the central channel. Perhaps you can visualize it as a single drop of water dripping out of a faucet or a tube. Once the drop of light has fully emerged from the tube, allow it to move out and away from your forehead to a distance approximately six to eight inches away from your physical body, allowing the drop of light to now grow into a larger sphere. It is kind of like blowing a bubble of light out of your forehead, allowing it to enlarge as it floats out and away from your body for this short distance.

Continue to visualize this sphere made of and filled with light and hold its position six to eight inches away from your third eye, the sixth chakra. As you prepare to move forward with the exercise, draw in a deep breath and allow your body to exhale that breath. You may even find yourself yawning. Yawning is the body's mechanism used to stimulate the releasing of blocked or unnecessarily stored energy in the body through the rapid infusion of life-force energy, prana.

At the peak of each yawn *see, feel, hear* or *know* within your mind's eye or intuitive feeling nature that the sphere of light is shattering into a million particles of light. In addition, if you have found, through your intuitive searching and cleansing of your body and/or energy field, that there is someone else's energy in your body and it is unwanted, you can use this exercise to send their energy back to them. It will release them in a more balanced way, dissolving their thought forms that have attached to you. Simply place within the sphere, prior to shattering it, the person, place, or thing that has been (incessantly) on your mind. Fill the sphere with their image and with God's light. When you are intuitively ready, shatter them and the sphere as you have done before. This does them no harm. It simply sends their energy back to them and they need their energy, fully intact, just as you need yours.

Once a person in workshop asked me if he could just let the sphere of light, with the person in it, float away. I responded by saying he could, but he would take the chance of them floating right back. By shattering the sphere of energy you quickly dismantle the energetic constructs that were attached to you, linking you to the other person or object.

Again, if you are thinking of someone, an event or thing over and over again within your mind, that is indicative of that energy being caught in your body. That is not necessarily wellness, for you or for them. This exercise will release that energy and that is why I recommend that you use it in conjunction with Running the Rainbow or the Spinal Chakra

Breath Work. As, for example, you are running second chakra, creative energy in either of these exercises, you may keep getting someone's energy popping into your mind's eye or feeling nature — even if you have not thought of them in years. They must have left an energetic impact on you or they would not be in your energetic face, so to speak, at this moment.

An important point to remember again is the meaning and depth behind your intention as you perform this exercise. You do not want to cause any harm or create any karma between you and someone else, but you have the right to own your energetic space without anyone else's unwanted influences in attendance. Therefore, as you use this exercise and encase someone or something within this sphere of light, oscillate or vibrate the light, sending them blessings and your intention of a healthy release.

Furthermore, this process will assist you in opening up not only the sixth chakra, your intuitive center, but to open all of your primary chakra centers as well. Simply follow the instructions as they are given above, only instead of forming the sphere of energy in front of the sixth chakra, allow the droplet of light to form within each of the chakras, front or back. Allowing it to grow, move away from the body and shatter it as you have done before. This is a very effective process for opening up your consciousness levels within all of the chakras. Play with it and have fun healing and balancing your energy.

Testing Your Intuitive Skills Every Day

One of the important factors that has brought success to students and clients over the years is that I share with them applicable techniques, not just theory. You have to get it into your body to really know what you are doing and have the experience, thereby building trust, faith and owning your power. Remember, again, your progress is going to be equal to your practice. I know that is a redundant statement, but there is a reason for this. I really want you to hold on to that affirmation. It is important as you develop yourself intuitively and spiritually, that you apply what you are practicing to your daily life — especially those seemingly mundane tasks.

There is a story about a young monk who was a newcomer to a particular monastery. Every morning the monks would gather at the central well to wash and bathe. It was this young monk's first morning at the well when he asked an older monk if the water from the well was cold. The older monk simply picked up a bucket of the well water and dumped it over the young monk's body without saying a word. The young monk got his answer through experience. The old monk was wise and knew that simply telling this youngster would not give him the benefit of the truer experience.

If you know and you do not do, you don't really know.

Incorporate these practices for building intuition into your daily life. They have been designed so that you can easily do that. Run Your Rainbow prior to an important meeting. Simply ask your body what color or combinations of colors it needs to move through it in order to be successful at your meeting, or any other endeavor you are about to step into. Trust the answers that your body's wisdom relays to you and Run Your Rainbow. As well, Run Your Rainbow and use the Sphere of Light technique afterward and clear your body, ridding yourself of unwanted energies and levels of consciousness that don't fit with who you are.

Go through the grocery store with your attention focused through your sixth chakra and choose your food from that perspective. Literally stand there at the produce section of the store and see what fruits or vegetable light up for you. Tune in and listen to the ones that call you. Or feel, literally with intuitive hands, which ones want to go home with you and nourish your body. If you do this regularly, the foods you choose and your eating cannot help but change because you will feel the difference between those foods in the produce section and say the chip and soda pop aisle. You will be able to discern the difference between the energies and consciousness of the fresher foods to the more heavily processed ones. Rest assured that your body can tell the difference. You and I have been so programmed by media and society regarding what to eat, we forget to listen to the body's intuition regarding what it needs. Begin to listen again. Your intuition can guide you in everything that you do, every step of the way. Your task at hand, as you develop it, is to simply listen, pay attention and commit to your intuitive wisdom in a trusting way, moment to moment.

6

The Mind

Where is yours when you're not looking?

The unceasing chattering of the mind has been an experience all humans can relate to. Spinning, seemingly out of control at times, the challenge is to master the chatter, master the mind — literally and energetically dissolving the chattering mind into a state of emptiness. I experienced this emptiness when I was in the throws of my near-death experience. I believe I entered into what is called the "Bardo" state of consciousness. During this time I experienced that state of emptiness described within the context of the *Heart Sutra*. I had *no eyes, no ears, no tongue, no body, no mind.* I had *no life, no death and also no extinction of them.* I was simply empty. A mind, a consciousness, rising and falling within what

I can only describe as a dark, velvety soup of universal consciousness. There was no fear, no attachment to the life I had left, nor any attachment to what might lie in front of me experientially or phenomenalogically. I was simply empty.

It has been both my experience and my observation that obtaining that state of emptiness while holding the form of a physical body, and while remaining immersed within the culture, takes practice and is indeed an art. Development of both the practice and the art of easing the mind's grip over your life is a worthy cause. As a healing facilitator one cannot let the mind run amuck while working with another's energy. Remember, energy is a byproduct or commodity of consciousness. Therefore, when I say work with energy, what I am really working with and referring to is another person's consciousness and the thought forms that weave themselves in and out of their present state.

It is not a good idea to be thinking about a myriad of other things while I, energetically, have my hands in someone's liver that may or may not be filled with disease. It is vitally important for anyone doing healing facilitation to stay present, for the client's sake as well as the facilitator's. Moreover, the state of centeredness and calm emptiness is the desired place to be. In my experience, by staying in and strengthening the consciousness and energy of the sixth chakra — the third eye — I can most easily access that place of centered calmness. You can achieve these states of emptiness, mindfulness, awareness and concentration through the practice of meditation, concentration or visualization.

Meditation is not what you think...

So many people say that meditation is extremely difficult or simply impossible for them. They think that since they cannot immediately still their minds they are not doing it right. As well, many find it difficult to still the body. Oh, how our culture has programmed us with a fast-food mentality. Not only do people feel they need to do it right, they put the added pressure on themselves to do it quickly.

However, the process of meditation is, in the beginning, to let the mind do what it will. Your task is to be the observer and simply pay attention to the ways in which your mind processes and operates. How else would you be able to obtain a state of emptiness if you do not understand the structure that your mind currently holds in the first place? Understand that each thought you have arises from the mind and sinks back into it, only to be replaced in the forefront of your consciousness by yet another thought or series of thoughts. Simply sit with these simple few ideas for a while as you read on. More will be brought to you through your practice and observations of the exercises included. Paying attention to your life's experience is the practice of becoming more mindful.

If joy and happiness are possible, why am I not thinking that way?

Understanding Thought Forms

I think, therefore, I think I am...I think? In the process of becoming enlightened, you will gain understanding regarding the source and movement of your mind, particularly your mind's thought, or thought forms. Thought forms create your reality. Like prayers or mantras, thought forms are charged with energetic levels of consciousness and certain emotional essences. This emotional charge is the catalyst for manifestation.

When I scan someone's body, I am always looking for disorder, imbalance and disease. In addition to scanning in that way, one of many foci is to pinpoint the thought forms within the cellular structure of the body, as well as the ones held within the energetic field surrounding the body. It is the thought forms, their location, directional movement and emotional charge(s) that indicate to me the depth and breadth of imbalance, disorder or disease. They are words and phrases that chatter away, subconsciously directing emotions, behaviors, biochemistry and a host of other aspects of human condition.

You can learn to tap into these thought forms, no matter how you gain access to your intuitive wisdom. One of my personal phenomena regarding access to intuitive information is that my *seeing* can be very molecularly oriented. That is the best way I can describe it. This allows me to intuitively track the directional movement of a disease, such as cancer, and thought forms either within the body or the energy field. I know that since I have been able to practice and hone my intuitive skills in this manner, you can also hone your ability to perceive phenomena at this level. Then, even more importantly, you need to move beyond the level of phenomena into unattached, unlimited consciousness. This is a matter of unlocking your limiting thought forms that restrict and bind you to a harder reality.

Sometimes you have to get there, before you get there...

The proper care and feeding of the mind, which brings about wellness — your God mind — takes time, discipline, self-awareness, persistence, displaying kindness to yourself and others and a deep awareness of the universal love that is yours to have and hold, always. You can be free of your mind's limiting beliefs, and your body's disorders, diseases and misalignments, if you commit to your wisdom and move forward from that place, one moment at a time. Simply hold the awareness of unlimited consciousness that is naturally within you. Remember you are an illuminating ray that shines from and is connected to the macrocosm — the body of God and the one pure universal mind.

When I look through my mind's eye at someone's auric field, what I see is really an aqueous of consciousness that surrounds them. All of your thought forms that are either holding your current constructed reality together or are bringing together new things by creating new thoughts, are floating in and around this field. In short, everything that is moving into or out of your life, as well as the thought forms that are creating your reality, reside within this aqueous of consciousness around your physical body.

Discerning where someone is on a consciousness level can be determined by a trained inner eye, so to speak, and by looking at the rate of vibration that makes up one's thought forms within their aqueous or energy field as well as the thought forms within the cellular structure of the body. People may say certain things about where they are, what they want in their lives etc.; yet, their life doesn't seem to be matching what they are saying. Why is this? It is because the thought forms that reside within their auric field, their aqueous of consciousness, do not match what they are saying.

It is not that they do not desire certain things — to lose weight, to make more money, to be kinder or a more mindful human being — it is because there are thought forms in the aqueous that are restricting the desired thought forms from creating a more solid reality. These thought forms are inconsistent with one another, oftentimes creating behaviors within your reality that are inconsistent as well. These thought forms can be created through your enculturation, imprinting and generally buying into what other people say to you or tell you to do. That is why it is important to understand the way in which your energy, your consciousness, runs through your body. You will be able to discern what is yours, what isn't and if it isn't yours, whether or not you still think it's OK to hang on to it. Do these current thoughts that run through your mind serve you? That is an important question to ask yourself from time to time, especially when you catch a thought that makes you feel out of balance or unwell.

The work you do as you dance your spiritual dance toward enlightenment, being assisted by these exercises, will allow you to identify and discern more clearly the thought forms that are creating your reality. Restating that which you desire to be more abundant within your reality and holding that thought form(s) above all others will create that which you seek.

In addition, as you move deeper into yourself, and the many facets of your life's experience, you will become more aware of the natural protocols that occur as you move forward, lifting your consciousness higher and higher. It all may seem a bit abstract and out of your normal range of context at first, but that is what is necessary anytime you try to experience anything new. You are stretching your consciousness, and when that occurs, you stretch the boundaries of your limited reality.

Enlightenment is easy — keeping it is difficult...

Remember to always stretch, for that is the way to enlightenment. That is the way to release all that has bound you to the hardness and the suffering that has occurred in your life. It is time to release the suffering and limited mind through which you have been perceiving your life. The attachment, the emotional attachments to the seemingly hard constructs that bind you in your suffering and pain — physical, emotional, mental and spiritual — will begin to dissolve.

You're Not Crazy — You're Becoming Enlightened

As a you move forward in your healing and growth, being guided by the maxims of whatever spiritually-based path you choose, you will come upon changes which, at times, are seemingly abrupt. When these abrupt shifts in consciousness occur they can sometimes throw you that all-powerful cosmic curve ball, making you question what you are doing and just where are you going with all of this.

We've all experienced it. There you are walking along on your personally prescribed yellow brick road to enlightenment. You are doing your meditations, prayers, prostrations, affirmations, internal and external conversations with those around you, in physical bodies or not. You're doing your ceremonies, hoping that reality will change as you glimpse other dimensions held within the universal aqueous of truth. You are there, engaged, struggling, skipping, and dancing down your path when suddenly you reach a segment of time in your life in which chaos ensues.

Thoughts stream through your head. Old crazy thoughts swirl in and out of your consciousness like tornadoes. What makes it worse is that these are same thoughts that have beaten you down, shamed you, cursed you and put you in a repressed and depressed state in the past. These are the very thoughts that you have been praying, prostrating and affirming away for the last seemingly millennium of time. These are the thoughts that you have been so dedicated to eradicating from your life.

You know the thoughts. The ones that say, I'm never going to get out of this situation. I'm clumsy and fat. I can't possibly take care of myself. I'm not allowed to be proud of myself. I've got to make enough to survive. I've got to keep my head above (financial) water. I'll never be able to quit this job and move into a type work that honors my spirit. Am I really a healer? I'm ugly. Should I just give up and stay in this marriage? I'll never be able to get it. I'm not smart enough and there isn't enough time or money to pursue what I want. I have other people to take care of. The abuse I suffer will always keep me bound. On and on they go, rattling around within your mind/body consciousness unceasingly ugly, unrelentingly loud.

Understand that when these thoughts arise within your conscious mind in such a torrential fashion, that is indicative of their lifting away from your body's cellular memory, as well as from the old constructs of your mind which created that reality. Willingly take in the fact that the work you have been doing has worked! You have danced your spiritual dance to release them, and you are in the process of succeeding in changing the hard bound reality that kept you shackled, and are smack dab in the middle of the process — creating your new reality.

You don't always catch the fact that this period of time, during which the cascade of thought forms pound you once again, is indeed indicative of these thought forms coming squarely into your face to challenge you and make sure that you are really ready to let go of them. They are there to say good-bye to you. Your job is to recognize this step within the natural stages of consciousness raising and let them go, with love and continued blessings for the lessons that they have bestowed upon you.

Once I had a young woman named Vivian in my office repeating a scenario that has played out many times with other clients and students. Vivian was a young woman, blonde, blue-eyed, a little over weight (her opinion), and angelically beautiful (my opinion). She had just taken a job in another city and was only at home with her husband on the weekends. She relayed to me that she had been positioning herself to leave her husband and her marriage for the last several months. She had created a new job, seemingly out of thin air. (The Gods above and her angels were listening to her heart's intention and assisting her in the creation of her new life.) She had also secured a place to live with some friends in her new city.

Over a time period of a few weeks, prior experiences with her husband had begun to shift. Her husband, who had periodic violent spells, was suddenly being nicer to her. Therefore, she was considering staying with him. "Well, if he's so nice and we're getting along now, why not stay?" This and similar thoughts would arise in her. However, she also knew that her husband's temperament had been chemically sedated. Nonetheless, the thoughts of staying kept coming up strongly and steadily, whirling around in her mind confusing her. After all, she had been doing her spiritual dance, holding her intention and attention on leaving and creating a new life for herself — a life of peace, spirituality and freedom. Even her life's experience was demonstrating to her the ease with which her new life was being created with her new job and new safe haven to live. Nevertheless, confusion, thoughts of staying and the truth of her new, exciting experience were all spinning around in her mind. I was witness to them, not only in her speech, but as I looked at her auric field while we talked.

She expressed to me her exasperation over the fact that she had been doing spiritual work: meditations, prayers, affirmations. Suddenly these thoughts that she had been attempting to transform, had been hounding her in an even more relentless form for the past few weeks. She stated to me that since she was having these thoughts of "giving in and staying" so often and heavily that maybe she should. She thought they might have been some divine guidance to stay. But her gut, her body was still screaming, "Go!"

I assured her that her divine guidance, nor yours or mine, would never suggest or demand through thought forms that she or anyone else stay in a situation or relationship that was abusive and heavy. That is not divinity at work, that is personality at a stage of growth releasing karma. As well, the tangible and rapid creation of mechanisms — her new job and place to stay — demonstrated support toward the new reality she was wanting to create. All of this illustrated that her path was indeed opening for her to step into a new realm of freedom. Those thoughts of "giving up and staying," were the very thoughts that had kept her in the marriage for so long.

Those thought forms were mechanisms used by her mind to keep her from moving forward with her life, implanted in her by the karma she had with the consciousness level between herself and her husband. These thoughts were displacing her personal perspective of her self-esteem, which had been whittled away due to her husband's abusive nature. That was her growth, to release and see herself in a new way.

I began to smile at her when she told me, once again, how she just didn't understand how she could be doing all this work and still experience these thoughts coming in so voraciously. Vivian stopped mid-sentence and asked what I was smiling about. Continuing to smile at her, I told her that her all the spiritual work that she had been doing was working. The voraciousness and heightened state of tenacity that these old thought forms were demonstrating were also demonstrating that they were on their way out, quickly. It was their last farewell. That is why they appeared to come forth so suddenly and with such strength. She had been doing all the right things. Through her spiritual dance she had created a new set of thought forms, reframing and therefore, transforming the old ones.

It is important to understand that you are the architect of your reality, building your erector-set of life through a variety of thought forms. Moreover, the understanding of the architectural components, along with the methods with which you dismantle and reconstruct your reality are important as well. In addition, I find it highly valuable to recognize what all of this looks feels, smells, and tastes like as you dismantle and construct your life every step of the way. It is obvious that when you want to remodel and rebuild your reality you have to create new space within your energy, your body and your consciousness (both subconscious and conscious minds).

For Vivian had been dismantling her thought forms and her life was being remodeled. The old thought forms were on their way out — out of her mind, out of her body — and their passageway, the way they could express to her that they were leaving, was to storm out of her body and her body's energy through her mind. Her task at hand was to recognize that since she had been so dedicated to her path of self-transformation these old negative thoughts were coming up to say good-bye to her. Secondly, her task was to let them go as graciously as possible. These are your tasks as well.

As you step toward your own personal enlightenment other things can occur, driving you crazy. Things get misplaced or lost, including you. Once I was traveling to the post office, a trip and route I take at least five time a week. However, at this particular time in my life I was in the middle of a nine-week meditation practice of periodic silence. I say periodic because I was still seeing clients and teaching, yet when I wasn't doing those two things, I was in silence and alone working on specific meditations and visualizations to lift my own consciousness. As I drove along this very predictable and usual route, suddenly, everything that I knew as familiar disappeared. I had absolutely no recognition of where I was.

I knew that I was on my way to the post office. I knew that I had just turned onto the street I usually do. Nonetheless, all the things along this segment of the path were strange and extraordinarily unfamiliar. Now, this happens to all of us occasionally. Yet, my experience was somehow different. The time in which I was in this state of unrest was rather long by my usual standards: five minutes or so. My state of mind began to grow more and more uncomfortable. Then the remembrance of my recent intention behind my practices came darting through my mind. My intention was to raise my consciousness through specific forms of practices. I realized that this loss of reality, although only lasting five minutes, was an indication that my work was effective. I settled into the fact that although I had no cognitive clue as to where I was, on some level, I understood where I was going simply out of habit and that I simply needed to accept what was happening. With laughter, I realized that I had been able to let go, for a few moments, the hard boundaries of my old reality, even its physical demonstration and form.

Incidents such as this may or may not happen to you, or they may have already occurred and you just assumed you were losing your mind. But if you are in the midst of a practice and walking your spiritual walk, most likely you are shifting consciousness, and not experiencing neurological or cognitive problem. (I am not making light of neurological or cognitive disorders that can cause biochemical shifts in the body, causing the mind to shift perspective. If that occurs, one should seek appropriate medical assistance.) Remember as you break through portions of your seemingly hard reality that all the things around you are just molecules that agree, for whatever reason or mode of attraction, to hang out and coagulate as certain forms and structures.

Years ago, I was applying corrective measures to a woman in my office. It was so long ago, her name escapes me to this day. Nonetheless, the experience has never slipped far from my memory. During this session, I was moving my hand above her left calf about four inches or so and was deeply entrenched in the process of shifting the molecular structure of her leg's energy when something rather odd occurred. Shockingly, a portion of her calf physically shifted right before my eyes. As I would look at her left leg, I could plainly see her foot, her ankle and her knee, as well as the rest of her body. However, the midsection of her left calf had turned into what I can only describe as a patch of energy consisting of grayish-white light particles, floating and moving very rapidly in current-like patterns. The sudden disappearance of this section of her calf and the physical manifestation of what I really believe we are all made of surprised me so that I literally jumped back. The whole experience lasted for maybe up to ten seconds. Not long at all. Nonetheless, I shifted thoughts that day regarding what was real and what wasn't. Because of that experience, I started even more diligently, on my work with molecular structure and its nature in regards to healing, energy medicine and the creation of reality.

Other things can occur when you are changing realities due to the success of your spiritual dance. Relationships change, and by this I mean your relationships with everything and everyone. Relationships naturally change because your inner relationship with yourself and your God source, in whatever form that is to you, is changing. Your relationships to your home, your family, your friends will change. They cannot help but do so. Even your relationship with items you possess, such as your clothes, will change. It will move beyond the "I can't find anything to wear" statement, which primarily arises from an ego state. To the "I can't find anything to wear" because it all looks foreign and fits your body differently. For when you do your spiritual dance, even if you are sitting still in thought, prayer, affirmation and meditation, your body's structure will change. When the practice is deep, the changes are reflective of that depth. Items in your closet will simply not fit for a while. No, this is not necessarily an excuse for you to go out and buy a new wardrobe, or furnishings for your home; however, you may find that the colors, styles and coordinates you were attracted to no longer hold a compliment to you and your new state of energetic being. Just be prepared, then you won't be so shocked when your relationship to your living environment and to your belongings changes. I find it funny how, over the years, my attraction to household items has changed. I live very simply now. And if I didn't have occasional guests over I wouldn't even have a chair or a couch.

All of the objects and people you have in your life have resonated with your energetic state and consciousness level. Now, after dancing your dance, you have literally changed the way in which your molecular structure vibrates, which is due to your intention, attention and newly created thought forms.

Therefore, it is natural that some of those objects and other relationships that you have resonated with in the past will not feel the same or even good any more.

You may start experiencing things such as losing your keys and the tools that assist you in moving your physical body through your world: your keys, driver's license, your day planner and things of this nature. They will suddenly disappear for a time, and then seemingly magically show up. When I went through the process of my divorce, I kept losing my driver's license. I could only laugh about it, because I knew that it was because I was changing the way in which I would move through the world. My license to move my vehicle was changing in name and in direction, so the temporary loss of my driver's license was not a surprise. In fact, I saw it as a positive sign.

Other events can indicate your shifting, even though you may think you're losing your connectedness. Guess what, you are. But only for a time. For example, I know a very gifted young woman who asked for my assistance regarding discovering the ways in which she communicated with others via her intuition. Lauren is very, very gifted, in seeing, hearing and knowing; yet, at the time, she was unsure of how to articulate her information. She had called to make another appointment and to talk about what she had been going through, and in her message she gave me several different phone numbers so that I could reach her. Her regular phone line was not working at that time. I tried several times to reach her through the numbers she had left, but to no avail. I saw her mother several weeks later and ask her to relay that I had tried to call Lauren, but could not get through. I told her that I thought it was really funny that her daughter was having trouble with her telephones, her mode of communication, as she also struggled with her process of communicating with her guidance and with others.

When things like this happen to you, lighten up and don't take it all so seriously. Life can sometimes be really tough, but your attitude — your thought forms — will either congest or clear a path for you. It's up to you. Oh, and Lauren? Currently, both her phones and her gifts are expressing her intuitive thoughts beautifully.

Please don't be surprised or afraid when your outer reality demonstrates the changes occurring within your innermost sense of self. That is the nature of nature. I often ask students how their meditations are going. I get all kinds of responses: confused, scattered, highly structured and ritualized, nonexistent, etc. I then ask them to think of their lives, and how they are currently going. They are amazed to grasp the fact that their current life's structure is a mirror of their meditation, or is it the other way around? A still mind is a still life. A chattering chaotic mind is a _____. You fill in the blank.

As you move forward on your journey, you will come to a time in your life when you will not have to dial up another psychic-hot line or anything else to discover what your future will be. Simply look into your mind and your energetic field. There you will discover where your thoughts are, where they are going, and at what speed. All will be indicative of your future. If you don't like what you see, feel, hear or know, change your thought forms.

Developing Discipline and Patience

The art of developing discipline and patience is like developing all other things — your progress will be equal to your practice. Unlike other forms of material processes, no one can start discipline or patience, and put it down to be picked up by another person. There is no assembly line in the personal development of spirituality or spiritual-like characteristics. You and only you can develop these characteristics which will lead you toward enlightenment and liberation.

Listening and following the Two Sacred Laws — commit to your wisdom and live in the moment — will most assuredly lift you toward a more disciplined and patience-filled life. Being committed to something helps create the space for discipline to occur, and if you are committed to your path and to your intuitive wisdom, discipline will follow your endeavors.

Laziness is something that needs to be overcome in order to create discipline in your life. You will never really be able to uncover your soul if you are lazy. When you are lazy you demonstrate your lack of commitment to yourself and you tend to doubt your ability to do whatever task you would like to accomplish. Beyond thinking badly of yourself, this behavior can also lead you to the pattern of speaking ill of others or putting blame where it does not belong. Placing blame on others boils down to lacking commitment to yourself , doubting your own abilities and displacing them onto an external source. Pull those thought forms back inside, and be accountable for yourself. Don't be distracted by negative thoughts or actions. Understand and see the good in yourself, a source greater than yourself and the good in the world around you. thinking in this manner while combining the truths set forth in The Two Sacred Laws — commit to your wisdom and live in the moment — are excellent antidotes for laziness.

You can more easily develop any good trait, like discipline and patience, when you think about its benefits and positive aspects. By thinking about the positive aspects of discipline, for example, you gain deeper understanding as to how discipline can relieve the suffering in your life. By the mere fact that you have an innate drive to end suffering in your life, these new thoughts will begin to shift the old thought forms out of existence.

To build character traits such as discipline and patience there are several ingredients that must be in place. Do have positive and helpful thoughts toward yourself and others. Do behave toward yourself and anyone else in positive and uplifting ways. Set your mind's course on feeling and knowing deeply the first two ideals, then demonstrate them in kind and beneficial ways that will assist others and yourself toward a life path that is joyful. If you want a happy life, use these types of thoughts in a consistent manner. Do this and you will find your pathway to liberation and peace. After all, if you want your home's floors to be clean, yet you don't sweep, vacuum nor do you bend over and pick up the litter, your floors, your path, will be filled with debris. Know what you want. Act out your thoughts through the resources that God and Spirit have placed before you, holding another's enlightenment and also your own as a goal. A clear path will joyously fall in front of you.

Created through the realization that we are all one, patience will bring you into a more peaceful place in which it will not be so difficult to be disciplined about your life. Patience is the antidote for anger. Patience will allow you to respond to aggression or the negatively charged emotions and behaviors of others instead of reacting. Understanding and experiencing gratitude fosters patience.

I have a friend Bob with whom, at one time in my life, I spent a lot of time. He had a kind heart, yet, through various life experiences he had shadowed his heart with anger and distrust. We were on an adventure in the desert one day when we came upon a beautiful and sacred bird that had been killed in the road. We stopped and took the bird into the desert and gave it a burial according to sacred traditions I had learned along my path. A day or two later while driving in the city, Bob said to me that that experience of honoring the bird in that sacred way was the first time he had ever felt gratitude.

I was actually taken back. Even though I attempted to hold no judgment and embrace where he was, it was hard for me to grasp the fact that he honestly believed that he had never experienced gratitude before. We talked further and through that conversation it became clear to me that having gratitude in your life's experience allows you to let go of what you "think" life is suppose to be like. It allows you to be free and let others be free as well. Gratitude dissolves anger, distrust, and jealousy because it opens your heart to the expansiveness of experience, and therefore allows you to release control over others, allowing them to have an open experience as well. Gratitude fosters patience.

Trust, Faith and Power

When was the last time you felt powerless? When was the last time you felt fear? When was the last time you felt alone in the world? If have felt any of those recently, or have felt them in the past I would like you to get out a piece of paper. On that paper, write these three words in this manner:

Trust

Faith

Power

Now put this piece of paper where you can see it all the time — on your refrigerator, on your computer monitor, on your bathroom mirror or any place in your house that calls to you (remember to use your intuition, even in seemingly simple situations). Look at those words for a moment. If you feel power, not power over someone or something but empowered, you own and feel secure in your concept of self. If you feel power in that way, you automatically have your faith — faith in yourself, faith in God, faith in what you are doing. If you have your power and faith, you have trust — trust in the outcome and that it will be for your highest good. You will also have trust in the universal support system that weaves its way throughout nature and life itself.

Conversely, if you don't trust in God, trust in yourself, or trust the sense of oneness, you won't have faith that all will be well. If you don't trust, and lose your faith, you will most likely feel powerless as well. The next time you feel powerless, lack of faith or trust, look at these three words in this order and do your practice, whatever that is for you. Go to the woods, the ocean or someplace in nature and observe the universal oneness that connects us all. Draw power from watching a river, a stream, feeling the wind, the snow, rain or sunshine on your face. Lie, belly down, on the land and absorb the power of mother earth as she too breathes in and out in her own way. Draw strength from your preferred source of God, your family, or your friends.

If there is no external source from which you can draw, draw from the truest source of all there is. Draw from the power that lies asleep inside of you. Close your eyes and focus your attention on your heart space. Feel the power inside shifting, spinning and churning. Through that experience of feeling, something greater than yourself move within your own physical body, a belief will form. A belief will form because even you cannot endlessly deny what you have experienced within yourself. You felt the movement of life-force energy that is greater than yourself. Connect that with your environment. Understand the experience of oneness. As you do this faith and trust once more will grace your life. From that, you will be empowered.

The Universal Support System

Sometimes, when you are alone (and you can certainly feel alone even within the context of a crowd, marriage or family) your mind can spin out and take you to all kinds of places. The time in my life when I first learned of the power of my own mind, I mean really got an intense look at my own mental processes, was when I was ill. Even though my family, especially my mother, was by my side as much as possible, I was the one in charge of my thoughts. I was the only one who could go into my body's pain and understand what it was trying to say to me. You too are the only one who can go in and *see*, *feel*, *hear* or *know* your own experience of truth. You are not truly alone, however. There is a universal support system that will always be holding you, in some manner, whether you are aware of it or not.

Once I was sitting by a pool's edge and noticed the undulations of the water and shadows of light as they danced across the bottom of the pool. The water and the way in which the light and shadows flowed supported each other's existence. It was mesmerizing and I was lost in the moment.

Suddenly, someone dove into the pool shattering the calm orchestration of the water, light and shadows. Chaos took over, yet I sat there, observing how, even though the water and its counterparts were disrupted and chaotic, there was still a strong sense of unity and support underneath the chaos. Slowly, without mishap or forgetfulness of their order in life, the water, light and shadow all came back to their calm undulating place.

This certainly demonstrated to me what I had observed in my own life's struggles. No matter what chaotic scene may be playing out, there is always a supportive system that knows the order of things. When I demonstrate patience in that support system, as well as faith and trust, all will be right again. My job is, as is yours, to gather grace through our chaotic times, always remembering the universal support systems that lie underneath our perceptions.

7

Approaches That Support and Clear The Mind

Calming the chattering mind seems to be a topic in the forefront when addressing the needs of both clients and students, and rightly so. For it is the thought forms that play a large part in creating our reality and how we view that reality, whether we perceive it as positive, negative or neutral. There are five general responses that your mind can have, regarding any given situation — hate, dislike, neutrality, like and love. There are variations of all these themes and, naturally, we can have more than one response or reaction running through our head at any given time. Nonetheless, these are generally the five from which we build.

I believe it is part of our journey to discover the depth and breadth of who we are as human beings. Therefore, we are likely to have a life filled with experience that brings forth the potential to deeply feel the wide range of emotions of which we are capable. After all, if we were not supposed to feel them, they would not exist. Yet, beyond feeling them and just having them run amuck through our mind and through our lives, we must master the mind and the emotions. That self-mastery will take you out of suffering and toward peace.

In order to do that, it is vitally important for you to get in touch with and express these emotions. You need to give yourself permission to feel your anger, sadness and grief to the depth of your soul and conversely feel the love, joy and gratitude that are part of your make up as well. Feel them, but do not necessarily express them in a way that will cause harm to another and create karma for yourself. When you have found the two ends of your personal emotional continuum, you can then begin the process of reframing those thoughts which do not serve you or others. Reframing your thoughts and not letting these negatively perceived thoughts run amuck will allow you to slowly move toward the center of your being. As you come towards that calmer unattached place within you, you will find even- mindedness.

It is in that centered place of even-mindedness that you will become more at ease and at peace with your interior and exterior world. It is in this centered realm where you will discover more clearly the purpose for which you are here, and how you can be of better service in assisting yourself, your loved ones and others.

These attendant exercises are simply a small example of what you can do to begin the process of calming the mind.

Let me say here as well, that as you begin or continue with your practice of meditation, be gentle with yourself. What you are really doing before you can bring calmness to your mind is to first understand the way in which your chattering mind works.

Look at it this way: before you remodel a building or completely dismantle it and start over, you first have to understand, clearly, the way in which the structure was put together and all the attendant relationships that occur within that structure. You need to understand where the structure's wiring is, and how that relates to the heating and cooling system, and how that relates to the plumbing and so forth.

Therefore, you can see my point regarding the helpfulness of understanding the workings of your mind and its particular way of being. All the exercises in this book will help you in that area. Within this particular section, you will be guided as to how to use your mind's awareness, not only in understanding some of its various processes, but how you can apply what you are learning and observing about your mind to other areas of your life. For instance, how you respond or react to certain situations and people when confronted by change or challenges. Where does your mind go? What are the thoughts that constantly enter your mind, thereby supporting the construction of your reality?

In addition, these exercises will guide you in calming the mind, releasing the chatter that builds up over time, and calming your emotions as well. With these exercises, it is helpful to take note of important revelations, yet understand that revelations are not what you are necessarily after. Exciting phenomena can take place while doing these types of exercises. Yet, what you are desiring is not a phenomenon. You are desiring a release from the bondage of suffering and ignorance. You desire release from the emotional attachment to people, places and events, which are causations of suffering. As you progress, you will release even the above stated desires and just learn to be with what is. You will learn to come into that place of even-mindedness and simply move with the ebb and flow of life as it surrounds you, but does not become or overwhelm you.

Calming The Mind and Emotions Through The Breath

This is the easiest practice for most when it comes to how to do it, however some people still find this difficult. I would suggest that if you are seasoned at the art of meditation or just a beginner, doing this type of meditation/concentration will ease the stress in your life by leaps and bounds. The goal is to calm your mind and emotions, and the process by which you do that is to put yourself in the place of the observer and simply watch your mind's antics as you proceed.

Simply sit in a comfortable chair, or you may take a formal sitting posture on the floor with your legs crossed. You may want to put a pillow underneath, allowing the hardness of the floor to melt away. A traditional meditation pillow (called zafu) is available at various stores or through catalogs, but an every day pillow or cushion will do just as well. Now that you have gotten your body into the basic sitting position, it is advantageous to sit with as straight a spine as you can. After all, you want all that wonderful energy/consciousness to flow freely through your body.

So now you are sitting there, looking good, feeling good about what you are about to undertake. Now, let go of all of that. Let go of wanting to do it right. Let go of looking good and sitting there on just the best zafu you could find. Or maybe it's your favorite pillow, and you have all kinds of emotional attachments to it. Whatever the feeling, just make note of it and let it go. Let go of all desires to perfect your practice. Just sit and focus on your breath as it moves in and out of your nostrils or your mouth, whichever is more comfortable for you. Watch and observe your breath and then watch and observe your mind as it comes in to do its dance and take you off your concentrated focus. When you notice that you are not focused on your breath any more and that your mind has got you thinking about what's going to be happening after you successfully learn how to meditate, just simply draw your attention back to your breath, without judgment or condemnation. Simply move your attention back to your breath.

If you are just beginning your spiritual dance I would suggest that you do this exercise for 3-5 or 5-10 minutes per day (sometimes twice a day). The stress relief you will begin to notice almost immediately. In addition, you will become much more aware when you are out of this more calm and balanced state. And guess what? You'll now know how to get back there within a few moments of simply focusing on your breath.

For those of you who are more seasoned meditators you already know that life is a meditation, yet, we all need some quiet and focused time of breath concentration now and again.

Again, for you beginners, start slowly and work your way up to any length of time you desire. Life is a meditation. Develop yourself to work in that zone, cook there, sleep there and do your life's dance from there. Now that is not to say that you will not be emotional or that your life is always smooth and calm. Remember this is a human life you are living. However, this type of meditative posture, whether you are formally sitting, standing or walking through your life, will give you a gentler perspective that is not so wrapped up in the illusionary drama of it all. Simply focus on the breath, moving in and out of your body...

Creating Prayerful Time

Because life can be like sitting in the front seat of a roller coaster with your hands off the security bar, it is a wise person who takes time out to pray. To ask God, Brahma, Great Spirit, Lord Buddha, your soul and/or the universal life energy, "What's up?" Time to connect, to pray, to ask for help and assistance on matters that are important to you is vital to help create balance within your being. You know that when you are upset, emotional and distressed, chemicals flood your body. When you are calm, peaceful, relaxed, chemicals flood your body as well. Therefore, it is easy to say that different chemical reactions, energetically and physiologically, flood your body constantly and are dependent on which way your emotional pendulum is swinging at the time. When you are distressed and the chemicals in your body are pouring into the bloodstream, muscles and organ tissues, it is a good time to reverse those chemically negative affects on your body and ease your mind. One of the ways in which you can do this is through prayer.

Prayer is a powerful tool in many ways. I certainly believe in the power of it, especially groups praying and holding similar thoughts together. When I was ill, my father was doing some work and having some fun up in a very remote part of Alaska. Being a minister/historian/ anthropologist at heart, my father always takes the spiritual /historical/cultural look at the world around him. When he got the call that I was ill and dying he told his traveling companion of my illness and the word spread through the village. He told me days later, after he arrived back in Ohio and was with me in the hospital, that the whole village gathered and prayed for me that night. That was the night I went blind, lost all vital signs and had the NDE, lying comatose for a day and a half. I feel strongly that the loving, prayer-filled energy coming from that group, from my father, my mother, other family members and friends pulled me back to life.

The power of prayer is miraculous — never doubt it. I'm certainly not going to tell you how to pray, or what to pray for. Those are deeply personal issues and requests. All I am conveying to you is to use this tool to get closer to the power that already resides within in you as a child of God.

Once I was doing a lecture in Minnesota at St. Catherine's College. I was sharing the stage with a dear friend and wonderfully, brilliant woman Kathy Hanoseck. Kathy has turned fundraising for non profits into a successful art form, assisting so very many people along the way. Kathy took the stage first and was talking about her life's journey and gave an example of one of her favorite prayers. When things get tough in her life, her favorite prayer is, "Aw, come on God!!" The audience roared. What a great prayer.

I remember one time in the very early 80's when I was dealing with learning how to manage all the colors and energy I was seeing around people. I stood on a rolling hilltop in southeastern Ohio, tears streaming from my eyes, yelling at God and saying, "I want to know who I am and do that for my service to others." I got a little indignant with God in those days. I guess I figured I went from life, to death, to life again, what the heck could I lose by demanding what I wanted? And you know what? I have found that When I mix emotions with my prayers and totally let go, allowing Spirit to move in and take over, the manifestation process happens really, really fast.

Another example of how prayer has manifested in my life, occurred two years after my decision came to leave my marriage. Unfortunately, due to circumstances, I had to leave quickly and leave behind my two children, who were 17 and 18 at the time. It was horrible for everyone, but I knew what I had to do. I also knew that within three years I would be reunited with my children. However, at the time I prayed this prayer the children and I were 1,800 miles apart. I have no doubt that this prayer left my heart and zoomed to God's ears.

The children and I had just been speaking on the phone to one another, my daughter Alicia, my son Christopher and myself. There was not a dry eye, nor unbroken heart in the bunch. I hung up the phone, just after promising them that we will be together shortly and that all will be well. I literally got down on my knees and yelled at God again. This time I brought in my angels and told them all that I just want to be able to take care of my children and myself and that I wanted all of us to be together.

That night I had a dream that I was settling into my new house and that my daughter and older sister were in the house with me, fixing fresh flowers in another room. I went into the dining room and sat down to call my parents on the phone. In the dream I was sitting while talking to my parents looking out a picture window, and gazing at a large tree in the yard.

Suddenly, I began to shake and quiver and an archway appeared in the tree that I was gazing upon. I told my parents over the phone not to hang up. I was having some kind of a vision and I needed them to stay on the phone with me. They said that they were here for me. The dream continued and I sat there and watched as, out of the archway that had formed in the tree walked a beautiful woman wearing a red dress with a long thin golden necklace around her neck. At first I thought it was Mary, the Mother of Christ, and asked if indeed she was. She said, "No, I am an angel."

She began to walk away from the tree toward a circle of highly charged energy. As she continued to walk toward the circle she raised her right arm and hand as if to look at a watch, which of course she did not have on her wrist. Telepathically she told me, "It's your time." With that she sat down in this highly charged circle of energy. My eyes darted back toward the tree and in the archway's opening stood another angel, dressed in a creamy color holding a trumpet. This angel was angled slightly away from me and just stood there, as if protecting the opening of the tree.

I awoke feeling refreshed and alive. Within 10 days, my life took a 180 degree turn and things moved in a direction through which I was able to soon have my children come and be with me. My prayer was once again answered.

Many, many times I have lifted my heart up to God and prayed. Your thoughts your heart's desire are awaiting you. You just have to let those in the ethers know what you want, pack a bit of emotion behind it and move your thoughts and thought forms in alignment with your desires. Then, stand back, watch and be grateful!

One more thing about prayer. Ask for what you want, need or desire. However, I would strongly suggest that whatever you ask for, ask for it to come into your life in a balanced way.

One day while I was out driving and doing some errands. I had just returned from a workshop in British

Columbia in which I had experienced those wonderful spiritual juices flowing through me. Needless to say, I was charged up and rearing to go with my life. I was excitedly telling a companion that "God and the universe can 'shift' your life just like that," snapping my fingers to accentuate my point.

Within an hour and a half I was experiencing a rather unpleasant situation. All the fluids in my body suddenly wanted to escape, and believe me they were coming out of my body in every direction. I lasted through this process at home for about 20 minutes, but then went to the doctor. This was just not normal. While at the doctor's office, making a mad dash for the bathroom, I fainted dead away. The next thing I remember was being loaded into an ambulance and carted off to the hospital. They did a series of tests and found that I was just dehydrated. No kidding! I stayed in the hospital overnight and was released the next day, feeling a bit weak, but overall fine.

A few days later I was chatting with another friend who had attended the training with me and told her what I had said about "God and the universe shifting things" and then what happened afterward. She laughed with me and said. "Well, Laura, you're going to need to learn how to speak more clearly. The Universe probably thought you said shit instead of shift." We both laughed, but from that time on I have learned to ask for things in a balanced way, articulating my requests clearly as well.

We could all share countless stories about the miracles we have experienced though the use of prayer. We have all experienced it, whether we recognize it or not. Just do it.

Pray. Stay humble. Question, yell, cry and smile at the Gods above and ask for what you need, want and desire. If it is true in your heart and in alignment with the thoughts and beliefs you hold, you will experience it as truth brought into your reality, seemingly like magic. What is also nice, and adds a nice balance to the mix is occasionally, without desire or provocation, say "thanks" to God and Spirit for all the beauty that surrounds you and is inside of you. There is nothing like waking up and walking through your daily life with gratitude wrapped around you, keeping you warm.

Releasing Mind Chatter

There is a simple way to assist you in releasing your mind's chatter. You can play with this practice alone or with a partner. Take ten minutes out of your day and let your thoughts roll from your mind and out of your mouth. Whatever thought comes to your mind, speak it. Let the thought that sits behind or connects to the previous thought rise up and be spoken also. One after another the thoughts will come rolling off your tongue. It does not matter if they seem connected to you or not. Just let them roll, no judgment, no self-counseling (if you are doing this by yourself), no fixing, stopping — just let go of your thoughts. The power of release comes in the vocalization of them — so speak up (pun intended). Lift up your voice, your emotions and intonations. Let your thoughts and voice join together to release the chattering that takes place within you. This practice shakes loose the chatter so that you feel refreshed and relieved afterward. Do this regularly to avoid mental build up.

If you do this with a partner, simply follow the above directions. As well, sit with your right shoulders slightly touching one another. The purpose behind this posture is that there is no space for judgment, consoling, fixing or pampering. No oohing, aahing or coddling actions. That is why you are sitting near one another, but not facing one another. The person speaking is doing just that, speaking. The person listening is doing just that, listening. Do this without any eye contact or physical touching to distract the speaker. The posture of the two partners is such that none of the vocalized energy from one person will "get on, or attach to" the other, as you will be facing opposite directions.

These are powerful tools to use in a partnership situation. It is intimate, freeing, and nonjudgmental. When you are finished speaking, you are finished. There is no going back and discussing what was said. It's over. Do not attach or hang on to anything that was said. You can do this practice in as little as ten minutes per speaker, or up to 30 minutes. It all depends on how much time you have and how much chatter you need to release.

8

The Body

*Just as hands and other limbs are thought of
as the body's members,
Shall I not consider other beings as the limbs and members
of a living body?*

Samantha

I was doing an assessment over the phone with a woman in the Southeast. She listened as I intuitively dissected one of the ovarian cysts in her body. The energy of this particular cyst was such that I could divide it up into three sections. Each section held energy that appeared to deal with various traumas that had affected her emotionally and behaviorally throughout the years. Each was energetically marked very clearly with a specific age indicating at what time in her life these traumas occurred. Furthermore, I noticed that relationships had been established with other parts of her physical and energetic anatomy (the chakras), as well as with her spiritual and emotional/behavioral anatomies. In short, all parts of her being were affected by these traumas to varying degrees. There were physical and energetic correlations throughout her body.

The far right section of this particular cyst held within it the emotions of anger and frustration. Both of these emotions were associated with her not being able to speak her truth from a very early age. This affected not only her second chakra where the cysts were located, but her fifth chakra, the throat. Chronic sore throats were a constant part of her life — symptomatic of repressed anger. As a child, she was not taught that it was OK to express anger, and therefore created an emotional/behavioral pattern that supported the stuffing down of her emotions.

The middle section of the cyst held within it deep sadness, and was the basis for her perceived inability to pursue what she really wanted to do. Within her energetic system, this issue was related to the age of three years old. I discovered the age relationship as I looked deep within her chakra system and saw a picture of her within my mind's eye as a three-year-old being told to hurry up and come along to do something else. Also encased within this picture were her feelings of simply wanting to be left alone to play with her toys. She told me that what I said made sense to her and that to this day she dislikes interruptions while engrossed in a task. Moreover, she told me that she doesn't allow herself much time, if any, to play and have fun.

The last section of this cyst held within it pictures of her not being able to do things right, as well as not believing in herself. This corresponded with the energy within her third chakra, a lack of self-esteem. These energetically charged, emotional patterns set the stage, producing fear around her and preventing her from being willing to try new things. However, she was tired of missing out on new opportunities. This particular energy, wrapped with these specific emotional reactions, affected her solar plexus chakra, resulting in having to experience and deal with a nervous stomach for many years.

Samantha's situation demonstrates the relationships that are fostered and maintained through the processes of energetic/emotional impacts and the emphasis they can have on the physical structure's level of wellness. Whether or not you have a full blown disease or are just feeling out of balance, there is a voice(s) encapsulated within your disease, disorder or misalignment. It is a voice that will direct you and allow you to map out the various impacts and causes of what is happening within your body. It is up to you, the individual, to intuitively guide your senses and mind inside to where your body's wisdom resides. Then listen, pay attention and act on the information provided.

Jonathan

One day I walked into my office and immediately saw the energy of a cancer- ridden body lying on my table. This man's body was so riddled with cancer that every one of his chakras was clogged with the energetic telltale signs of cancer — black, concretized, sticky energy. I saw a most gentle and luminous soul lying there as well. Nonetheless, the energy field that surrounded his body told me that it would not be too much longer before he would make the transition from this world to the next.

Within the exterior of his energy field were the ever-so-common vacant spaces created by the lack of energy, which creates physical matter. I have seen this condition, time and time again in my work, especially with those in preparation for transition. His exterior energetic system, which had supplied, as well as created, his physical body with life-force energy and sustenance was melting away, similar to the way in which sugar dissolves in water. Just about all I could do for him was hold him, smooth his energy field and talk.

We talked about his fears and concerns about what he was leaving behind. I did a gentle assessment regarding what I found in his body which may have lead to the cancer — his holding on to deep hurt and resentment for decades. He wanted to know what I saw so that he, in turn, could do whatever he needed to do in order to clean up his business with family and friends. We talked softly about such things. I held his vital force energy in my hands and prayed for him. I shared with him some of my experiences on the other side with the intention of easing his fear of death. He was tired of being in pain, physically and emotionally. He was also afraid that death would hurt. I told him that, based on my experience, there is a point during the illness when the pain leaves and there is nothing but peace at the end. I heard a month later that he had crossed over within a few weeks of our visit. His relatives told me that he had died peacefully, at home with family and friends. I felt blessed to have known him.

Barbara

A charming woman lay on my exam table. She had been suffering from bouts of asthma for many years, as well as recent frustration over her work within a particular bureaucratically-based system. During the assessment process, I placed my hand on her chest over her thymus gland, and asked her why there was such deep sadness and emotional constriction for her around the age of four. "What have you been disowning about who you are — your truer nature — since that time?" I asked.

Tears, which had been held back too long, loosened and began running down her cheeks. She told me that she used to see lights and sparks of colors dance outside her bedroom window at night. She knew they were guides of some kind, her very special guides, trying to relay information to her. She also knew that she knew too much about Spirit, about God, and that the family in which she had been born into would not tolerate a young child who had so much intuitive, spiritual information. As a result, she shut down. The lights and feelings of interconnection with God and Spirit seemingly left her.

From that time on, she began to grow into a four foot, 11 inch tall bulldozer, (my term for her) which helped her manage her life from a point of view different from her more intrinsic level. By rearranging the way in which she interacted with her inner self, her family and the world around her, she began her inaugural journey back toward reopening to herself and to her truer power. She has since been in the process of rediscovering her incredible intuitive healing abilities and marvelous artistic gifts. It only took her forty some years to tell someone that part of her life's story, a drop in the bucket compared to her soul's existence.

Jennifer

A school bus? Now what does a school bus have to do with this woman's neck and her broken collarbone? I thought to myself as I dug further into the recesses of my intuition. "Now don't think this is too weird," I said to Jennifer, a first time client, "Did you ride a bus to school around the age of five?" (The age of 5 came up because I was intuitively seeing that there was a relationship between the school bus, her neck, age five and a pattern around inhibited communication — that it had been locked in her energetic, emotional and behavioral being since that time.)

Our session continued and we discovered some interesting things that related to the inhibited communication patterns that she had been working on, as well as issues around her broken collarbone. However, later that evening, Jennifer called me and left a message that brought the "school bus" back into the forefront. She told me a few details concerning a conversation she had had with her mother after our session. She included in her conversation with her mother what I had said regarding the school bus and that her emotional issue(s) around the age of five were connected to both the school bus and the restricted energy in her neck.

Jennifer said in her message to me that her mother started laughing when Jennifer told her of the school bus popping up in our session. Her mother asked her, "Jennifer, Don't you remember your first day of school?" Jennifer told her mother that she didn't remember. Her mother reminded her that on her first day of school, at the age of five, she had fallen asleep on the bus and ended up staying on it past the school drop-off point. She missed her entire first day of kindergarten because of it. When the bus driver came back at noon, she was startled awake. She may not have remembered that experience consciously, but the energetic, emotional and behavioral aspects of her body did.

David

A young man of eighteen lay on the examination table in my office. We had been in the process of assessment for several minutes when I placed my hand on his liver and said, "The sugar and caffeine from the chocolate candy you ate yesterday are still rolling around in your liver, making it work a little harder than it wants to." He looked up at me with his eyes and mouth wide open and said, "How do you know I ate chocolate yesterday?"

In what direction do these and the countless other stories I could share with you point? Does the phrase, "You are what you eat" hold any meaning for you? We have all heard this phrase at one time or another, and that simple statement is true enough. As a medical intuitive it has been my experience that we are, indeed, what we eat — and a whole lot more. We eat in an attempt to nourish our bodies, our emotions, our minds and our souls in a variety of interesting and creative ways.

You literally are the author of your anatomy. You have constructed your body, over time, through the innumerable events and encounters with people and other forms of stimuli that have entered into your life and energetic field. Your body, your life and the emotional and behavioral components with which you manage your world are all interrelated energetic patterns resulting from events that have first left their imprints upon your energetic system — your chakras. It doesn't matter whether the imprinting process results from a traumatic experience or a joyful one. It is the way in which you hold onto the situation and/or to the memory — emotionally, behaviorally, and especially energetically — that matters. And the way in which you hold onto something depends upon the way in which you perceived what happened to you in the first place.

The memory bank of experiences you possess, based on the people who raised you, whomever you went to school with, played with, made love to, married, gave birth to, worked with, etc., assists you in writing both your energetic and physical body's story. All of these stored memories are actors, so to speak, assisting you in both the writing and presentation of your anatomy. As you move through your life and through its myriad of experiences, these actors interact with your energy, rehearsing and performing the lessons you are here to learn, as well as the lessons you are here to teach others. Furthermore, those to whom you have given the authority offer their perceptions and belief structures to you, and, most likely, you take them on. You have, as we all have to a large degree, authored your anatomy based upon the perceptions and belief structures of others, namely our culture.

While this is not necessarily a harmful or bad thing, it is important to know whether or not these learned perceptions still serve you within the context of your current life or state of being. Take a thoughtful look inside of yourself for a moment. Have you been authoring your anatomy, and therefore your life, based on someone else's truths? And if so, how much so? And do these truths serve you? Do they honor who you are, or what you want to become?

In order to remain relatively civilized within a specific culture we need to find the balance between two cultural poles. These poles are, at one end, the group cultural mind. At this end, the individual and his or her individuality are totally lost within a sea of cultural consciousness. The other end is that of the individual maintaining his or her existence in a hermit-like manner, away from all of the culture's precepts, morals and values. In most cultures, people are taught that we are responsible for both constructing and maintaining that culture. Granted, to some degree, we need be able to comply with our culture's norms and mores in order to avoid chaos. For it really is an excellent idea for the inhabitants of this earth to cooperate with one another and behave in a manner that befits and benefits our existence. Hopefully, that will soon become a sustainable existence within this ever-growing global culture.

Yet, on other end of that spectrum we feel as if we need to honor and to be honored for who we are as individuals. In order to be that individual, it is imperative to know and to understand what our personal inner truths are, and how we can fit into the culture, in its present form, and maintain our personal, soul-based sense of integrity. It is about balance between the internal authority and the external authority.

Therefore, it is easily understood that one way for you to find balance in your external world as an individual is to find the balance within your internal world first. In light of that, do you know what your inner truths are? Your inner truths, when realized, will assist you in establishing this internal balance. The larger culture and its various institutions have done their job of bringing you up as a model citizen to the best of their abilities (whether you agree with them or not). However, what you have been taught as truth, and what you deeply believe may be slightly askew or even far removed from the deeper, more internal truths of your soul. It is time to look deeply into what you believe about yourself, your world and the way in which you move through it. For the way in which you move through your world — energetically, emotionally, spiritually and physically — genuinely creates every part of your body's cellular structure. Your internal doctrines, or truths, whether they are realized or unrealized (conscious or unconscious) manifest into your actualized external doctrines. These internal doctrines then weave the very fabric of your being, creating a tapestry-like script of your life and your body.

You are, indeed, the author of your anatomy. Everything you do, think, feel and know determines the health and nourishment of your body, as well as feeds or starves your soul. With this being said, I have yet to meet a disorder, dysfunction or disease residing within the human body that does not have emotional-behavioral components attached to it. The nourishment you have given or allowed yourself to receive, or lack thereof, is most definitely evident within the energetic core of the disease.

Through assisting people as a medical intuitive, I have been privileged to work with a wide variety of the diseases and disorders that currently plague humankind — cancer, fibromyalgia, chronic fatigue syndrome, digestive disorders, candida, panic attacks, diabetes, spinal issues, respiratory disorders — the list goes on and on. All of the people who I have assisted in dealing with these disorders and diseases have had a variety of emotions packed inside of them at the point of disease, or what I call the point of "emotional/energetic congestion." The evidence of these emotions, along with the behavioral patterns, tells both me and the clients that they have been either holding or losing their life-force energy in regard to a particular situation, traumatic experience or person in their life. In addition, it is most likely the case that these issues have been affecting them for some time, and in some instances they have been stuffed down inside them for years and years. Somehow, within the rush of containing and maintaining our fast-food mentality culture, we have forgotten to nourish our soul.

Each of us is born with an intrinsic energetic pattern that is a clear reflection of the soul's purer nature. However, as we move through our lives absorbing one experience and then moving on toward another, we begin the process of redirecting, overcompensating and rerouting this intrinsic pattern. We form a new one that allows us to manage our lives based on the information and experiences we are receiving from the external source of authority. Those external sources are our family and the various institutions within the culture — religious, educational, governmental and economic. Conformity and appeasement are commonplace in our society, and those types of behaviors, along with the suppression of emotions, cause untold numbers of problems.

A situation that is problematic and core to the manifestation of disorders and diseases is that we often ignore our soul's voice, a voice that is directing us toward our gifts and talents. Instead, we go off to become accountants, plumbers, teachers, factory workers, bankers, or parents because it is the right thing to do or it's what our families wanted us to do. Some are born to be in these professions, some aren't. Over the long haul, however, it is unhealthy to do something for a living for which, intrinsically, you are not suited. Your living does not make you who you are, even though the culture says so at this point in time. You must figure out who you are and then, if you want to, do who you are for a living. After this is accomplished, you will live a much more rewarding life, affecting yourself and your environment in a conscious, soulful manner. Note the following statistic reported in various morbidity and health studies: Americans have more heart attacks at 9:00 a.m. on Monday morning than any other country's population on this planet. It appears as if people have totally disconnected from their heart's desire, and their intrinsic energy pattern, to become and to do something they are not.

Over and over, I have seen prostate and colon disorders, as well as hemorrhoids, that are the result of early childhood imprinting from the parents who are dealing with the memories of the great depression. This holding onto a fear-based reality is in reference to the lack of money — to the lack of safety surrounded by the fear of survival. Money is, within the model of the chakras, a second chakra issue. However, within our culture many people place their issues about money within a survival context — a first chakra issue. Therefore, first and second chakras can be affected in cases such as these, a clear case of authoring your anatomy. Many people have built their whole life on this fear of lack. A life built on any fear is simply not a good idea. I have seen clients who are very successful in life and in business who are still, based on this early programming, squeezing the life force energy out of their first and second chakras, causing these types of illnesses.

In female clients, I have seen many diseased ovaries, breast cancers and dysfunctional thyroids due to the convoluted issues and distorted internal pictures regarding body size, creativity, abuse, the inability to own and then speak their truths, as well as issues around sexuality. All of those cultural directives can result in shutting down each respective chakra. Holding in emotions such as deep hurt and resentment along with brokenhearted dreams damages the heart chakra, paving the way for breast cancer and heart disease. I have seen the patterns over and over again. We must get a handle on all of this and get back to our intrinsic nature, whatever that is for each individual:

Illnesses Are Signals from the Soul

There are natural laws within the universe that, as far as we know within our human existence, will never change. These include for instance, the law of cause and effect — karma. It is upon these laws that all things within the universe can depend. These universal laws are within our human bodies, the internal universe (the microcosm), as well as the external universe (the macrocosm). Another law, or truth, of the universe (both micro and macro) is that all structures are made of energy and have mass. As well, the energy that constitutes a particular mass has a vibrational rate, which supports, and therefore, identifies that mass. This arrangement supports the fact that vibrational rates vary from constructed mass to constructed mass. An example taken from within the context of the earth's body is that the molecular structure of rock vibrates at a different rate than that of water. Also, within the context of your body, your bones' molecular structure vibrates differently than that of your blood.

With that being said, and in reference to your body's mass, if there is a misalignment within your body's system, a vibration will be set up that is not within the normal range of your body's structural and energetic vibratory range. That discordant energy and vibration will announce the fact that something is wrong, something is out of harmony. This principle is how I can tell when a part of the body is out of harmony with the surrounding tissues or structure of the body — I can *see, feel, hear* or *know* the variants within the body's vibrations. So can you.

Here's a little story, which tangentially illustrates this point. My sister Christine and I were doing some traveling in Northern Arizona, and checked into a hotel near the Petrified Forest. The young man who assisted us in checking was of Native American descent. We had a brief, and interesting discussion about spirituality and the oneness of all things. Later that evening, Christine wanted something to drink and went downstairs and outside of the building to get a soda. Once at the machine, however, her attempts were unsuccessful. One of her dimes simply would not work. The machine would not accept it no matter what she did. The young man who helped us check in walked over to see if he could be of any assistance. Christine gave him the dime and he placed it in the slot, only to have the same result. The dime slid down inside the belly of the machine, and plopped out into the coin return. After a few attempts, he calmly picked up the dime, handed it back to my sister and said, "This dime is not in harmony with the machine." He smiled and walked away.

The machine, of course, is the structure. It is your body, your energy or your life. The dime can be anything or anyone who comes into your existence and slides right through not offering any service to you, and possibly causes your body's energetic vibrational rate to be out of harmony. Whatever or whomever your dime is, it is important for you to see why something you are attempting to put into your body or into your life is not working. Moreover, it is important to know why is it not in harmony with what you need or desire.

When it comes to the human condition, your soul's health is echoed through the various systems and chambers of your physical body. By listening deeply to your body and to your soul's voice, you can locate your source of disharmony. Your soul is the signal maker. Your body's pain is a result of your soul's signal making. This pain is associated with the disorder(s). This disorder is the noise — whispering, chattering or screaming. In brief, your body is the mouthpiece through which the soul's signal is heard.

Being in service as a medical intuitive and healing practitioner has shown me that, more often than not, disorders and diseases are due to a person going against innate truths, going against their soul's voice. Your soul's voice is accessible intuitively, and that is why it is so important to develop a practice that fosters this type of intuitive connection inside of you. However, if you haven't been taught to honor your intuition, how can you hear your soul's cry for help? This is a problem!

Once I had a phone client who called me wanting an appointment. Wendy was crying and emotionally distraught. She told me how she had been through a cavalcade of physicians over the past few years — allopathic, naturopathic, and homeopathic physicians. Some of the physicians told her to take particular herbal formulas and that if she did so she would be well in a matter of weeks. Some doctors told her to go and get some blood test done and get a CAT scan. She went back and forth with the more alternative-oriented doctors, as she was afraid of going to get more invasive types of tests. However, Wendy's condition was worsening. After this long drawn out process, she didn't know what to do, and so she finally sought out my assistance.

As we talked, I brought up a discussion about the definition of holistic. I shared with her my point of view, which is that sometimes when you are ill herbs can be the perfect remedy. However, sometimes you need castor oil packs, sometimes meditation, sometimes you need traditional methods of diagnosis and sometimes you need surgery. I asked her what her body had to say about what she should do. Wendy didn't know because she had never asked. I suggested that she ask and see what wisdom her body had to share with her.

Although I didn't do a formal reading, as we were setting up an appointment time, I suggested to her that she talk to her stomach area. There was a tremendous amount of energetic activity there — a lot holding, fear and anger. Wendy called me back a week later and to my surprise, her voice was joyful and filled with elation. She told me that when she talked to her body, and listened to it, it told her to go get the CAT scan, along with some more traditional tests. She did just that. Mind you, this woman's voice was filled with joy as she told me the results of her tests. It may seem odd that the results of her tests showed that she was heading toward the advanced stages of stomach cancer and that she had only a 33% chance of survival. The beginning of her healing was in the knowing, and the new connection she had begun to foster with her body and the emotions it held.

You may hear these cries coming from deep within you, yet not know what they are about. At times these soul-level pleas become so muted that they end up being pushed down even further inside where you can't hear them. Over time you move so far away from your inner source, your soul may seemingly not even know who you are anymore. When this occurs, energy, thoughts and emotions begin to grate against the core of your being, creating, what I call psycho-physical dissonance and energetic disharmonies. These conditions slowly grind away at the physical body, affecting your outer reality. As I have seen over and over again, we will become ill, sometimes deathly ill, if we don't start listening and acting upon our soul's voice and its directives.

Illnesses, as you know, do not have to be physical in nature. It is, however, an effective way for your soul to get your attention. For when we take a deeper look into these components of illness, they serve as keys which can assist us in unlocking the mystery of how our thoughts, emotions and/or our behavioral lifestyle may have affected the creation of the illness. When we understand the depth and breadth of what has brought us to a certain place, we are much better able to handle the situation and therefore step more powerfully and solidly toward a resolution. Again, understanding the structure of your life is essential.

Here is one client's story, which stunningly illustrates how emotional and mental perceptions influenced behavior as well as this person's intrinsic energy system which, over time, caused disease. Mary Beth arrived in my office wearing an oversized red sweater, which had a huge black heart on it. The black heart on her sweater was so big that it covered her from the top of her chest to her abdomen. (Talk about a signal from the soul; even her choice of clothing for that day reflected the state of her soul.) We got to know one another for a few moments, and then I began the process of energetic assessment. She had told me that she had been suffering from severe endometriosis for several years and that she had been through all sorts of traditional medical hoops with no relief. Her alternative in that arena was surgery — which was something she hoped to avoid — hence her visit to my office.

In brief, what our session consisted of was this. With her permission, I placed my hand on the outside of Mary Beth's body where her left ovary was located. Immediately, a picture of Mary Beth came into my mind's eye. In this picture she was her current physical size and shape; however, energetically she was of a much younger age, perhaps around the age of eight. In other words, I saw her as an adult, with the energy of a child, lying in a fetal position and weeping. The emotional energy around her left ovary, as well as this energetic picture I was getting, was one of deep sadness and sorrow. There was, in addition, a tremendous amount of deep hurt and self-pity wrapped around these physical and energetic components. All of this was jammed into the tissue structure within the reproductive area of her body. The lack of self-esteem and powerlessness in reference to her being a woman was most evident as well. Physically, based on the way in which I see, there were several cysts on her left ovary and distorted tissue that had been stretched and pulled. The tissue appeared to be contorted, as it had been twisted and locked up over time to match the energy and emotions she had kept bottled up inside her for years.

The energy and physical state of her right ovary was very different from her left. On her right side the emotions were that of deep seated anger and resentment, toward herself and toward others in her life, particularly the men with whom she had formed intimate relationships. Especially evident and bundled up energetically within these relationships was, again, her perception of her own powerlessness. All the men in her life, from her father on, including her two husbands, were represented. Again, based on the way in which I see, the cysts on Mary Beth's right ovary were like mini volcanoes, seething and spewing emotional and energetic toxins out into abdominal area of her body. There was a lot of work to be done, and the great thing about it was that Mary Beth was really ready to take back her body and life, and rewrite her anatomy.

Within a few months her pain was gone, the cysts were healed and Mary Beth had a new perspective on life. She had truly devoted herself to her spirit. A spirit that was calling to her from within her body's pain. She listened, acted and healed herself.

Truth is always present, although sometimes unnoticed...

Illnesses are signals from your soul, telling you to go deep within yourselves. Illnesses beg you to start listening to the real source of your being — your soul's voice. It is a voice of innate wisdom that will lead you toward the life we are meant to live. It will lead you to the place upon this planet where you are meant to dwell. Moreover, it will guide you to the people with whom you are meant to be with and who can surround you with love.

The Writings of Your Soul

Your inner book of wisdom, the writings of your soul, exists in a reality that is oftentimes much different than the physical body and external reality you display outwardly, which is based on your socially constructed mindset and perceptual beliefs. The writings of your soul are deeply encoded inside of you. They are, nonetheless, accessible. The entire natural wonderment of who you are, along with all of the talents and gifts that you have brought into this lifetime are contained within these writings. These innate components of who you are projected out into the world through your intrinsic energy pattern, as you embody these talents and gifts for the benefit of humankind. They are uniquely yours, as we all have our own energetic blueprints, so to speak, with which to work and display our talents. These talents and gifts you possess, which are encoded within the writings of your soul, are spoken to your inner self through your heart.

When I was in the depth of my near-death experience and on "the other side," the communication I had with those that were there with me took the form of heart to heart communication. There were no vocal interactions in the way in which we think of them. Everything that was expressed was from one soul to another through the heart center. You came into this world with this same level of openness in your heart center. Just look at the openness and heartfelt expression that children offer to the world. However, somewhere along life's route, maybe your openhearted manner of expression got rerouted. When this rerouting takes place, for whatever reason, you can gradually begin to lose the connection with your intrinsic energy pattern, your soul's internal doctrines, which speaks through your heart center. As a result of this loss, to whatever degree it has occurred, you can lose sight of your innate talents and gifts. Unfortunately, I am often witness to this type of disconnection when I work with people in the office or on the phone. Even if they are usually joyful and pleasant people, helpful and kind, on deeper, private levels, their heart centers have been hurt along the way and closed down to varying degrees as a protection mechanism.

Oftentimes I see energy that is being held within the body that is the result of something that happened to close this openhearted nature. This affects the way a person expresses herself for various reasons, which usually boils down to a self-created myth that says it is no longer safe to be who you intrinsically are. When you close down the heart chakra, or any other chakra of your body's energetic system, it ends up redirecting your intrinsic energy pattern — a pattern that previously involved a primarily heart-centered openness — into a new energetic pattern. This new pattern is a way to manage your life, yet it does not connect to this deeper aspect — moreover, the grasp on your talents and passion to express them dims. Over time you get used to the dimness, and it becomes a part of who you are. You may tell yourselves this new way is tolerable for the most part. I say that it is no longer tolerable. It is time to rewire ourselves, every one of us, which will allow ourselves to be taken back to our intrinsic energetic patterns. There you and I can begin to utilize our soul's writings once again.

For example, a male client, Paul, had been working in the technology field for several years. He faced a long commute each day, only to sit in an office that he hated. He had managed to create a schedule in which he works one day of the week at home on the computer, but there was still a great deal of pain and suffering in his emotional heart as well as his physical body. As a result of his being tolerant of his situation, and the way in which he had chosen to manage his rerouted energy, he had lost his vitality and passion for life. When asked, he revealed that what he really would like to be doing is writing and audio-taping children's stories from a spiritual perspective.

During our session together it was very clear that, through his socially constructed reality, Paul had rewired himself in order to manage his life a little better, or so he thought. He had completely rewired himself and his energetic system in order to fit into a mold that somebody else had made for him — his father. Now no blame should be placed on his father, as we all have a soul-level role in every interaction we encounter. Paul's issue was that both his physical and energetic prowess were leaving, quickly. He needed to get his vitality, passion and energetic system back in alignment, and that meant he needed to do some inner work.

I want to describe to you what his intrinsic energy pattern was, but first let me expand on the workings of these patterns in general. Again, we all have a unique way in which we access, process and display our energy. We use the seven primary chakras when it comes to our intrinsic pattern. The chakras light up, so to speak, in different ways and in different orders, based on who a person is on an intrinsic level — a soul level, if you will.

Given that, Paul's intrinsic pattern was as follows. The energy came into his body first through the sixth chakra, the intuitive center (he was and is extremely intuitive, but didn't at the time of the reading know how to access or use this to his benefit). Next, and this is virtually a simultaneous occurrence, his intuitive center's energy flowed down to his second chakra, his creative energy center located in the lower abdomen. That accumulated energy then dropped down even further to his tailbone, the first chakra, which fed this area with energy. This flow of cumulative energy then sat in the first chakra lighting it up, so to speak, and made him feel comfortable and safe (first chakra is primarily about survival, safety and foundational support). After fueling the first chakra, the energy moved up the body's energy channels and into his heart chakra. At this point, it was as if his energy was checking in with the writings of his soul to make sure he was in alignment. Then the energy would spread a great deal of joy throughout his entire body. The core of his energy then moved from the heart chakra up into the throat chakra where the energy of what he was working on could be expressed, to others and to himself. Finally, after expressing this intuitively-based creative, secure, heartfelt energy, it all sank into his power center (the third chakra) where his self-esteem was nurtured and empowered. This gave him a strong sense of self-confidence. His seventh chakra energy was more like a frame for his entire body, as it wrapped all around him, feeding him from every angle.

Paul is a very spiritually directed person, as demonstrated by the above description of his intrinsic pattern, but he had been running his life as far away from this intrinsic pattern as he could get. If you recall, intrinsically, his sixth chakra (his intuitive center) was the center which naturally wanted to lead his energetic parade, his most natural and appropriate perspective on the world, and his third chakra was basically the last in line. However, during the session I had discovered that he has been running his life with his third chakra leading the way. He was out of balance. His life's dime was not in harmony. As a result, his body's health and his energy level had been slowly declining for years.

It is important enough for me to stress once again that in order to discover the writings of your soul, you have to get in there and look through the patterns of your life and see where you are not honoring your soul's doctrines. You have to be your own archaeologist and dig up your hidden treasures. You need to look at how you may have rerouted yourself and your energy to please, appease and placate others just to get by. When you begin to decode the graffiti within you there is a step that you need to take, and the awareness of this step actually comes quite naturally. You need to quiet your mind and go to the inner quiet place where the doctrines of your soul reside. Everyone has a place such as this. You'll find it as you do these exercises.

Let me also qualify what I mean by "graffiti." It is a term I give the socially-constructed inner writings that have been painted upon your soul's walls, so to speak. We all have it. You cannot live within a culture and not have it. Even iconoclasts have it. You will recognize, if you haven't already, that your graffiti is bouncing off the walls of your mind constantly. In order to cut through it you've got to begin the practice of stilling the mind/body chatter. Once you begin this process you will naturally begin to see your graffiti, the internalized vocal patterns that repeat themselves over and over in your mind. When this happens it is like a big neon sign goes off in your body. You recognize the fact that this graffiti-like chatter is not really yours to begin with. You've been holding it for someone else. While that is a very generous act, you don't need to go there any longer. It's time to sort it out and move it out of your mind, body and energy patterning. Your practice of quieting the mind is the beginning process for this and discernment will follow, allowing you to wipe off the graffiti from your soul's walls.

There is a posture in the practice of yoga in which you are standing on one foot with the other foot either placed high upon the front of the thigh or the inside of the knee. It is call the Tree, or Vrikshasana (Sanskrit). If you do this posture with your mind racing at the usual hundred miles per hour with your inner graffiti flying hither and yon, your balance will be affected, and the tree (you) will fall. A still mind is a still body. Likewise, a chattering graffiti-filled mind, as well as an undissected mind, is not going to allow you to progress along your chosen path in life either clearly or rapidly.

What is on the other side of your mind...

If your mind is not relatively still, you will not hear your body's voices which enable you to hear the whispers of your soul's writings. As this hindrance grows and continues, you will most likely begin to acquire excesses in your life. These excesses may manifest as added stress, added weight, too many people telling you to do this or that, or you may just start collecting objects in order to feed your starving soul. To get rid of the excess in your life you need to move through the mud of your mind, listen to your body's pleas and take a conscious look at the interior walls of your soul, upon which the cumulative graffiti of your socially constructed life's script has been scrawled.

Decoding Your Inner Graffiti

Move beyond your current understanding of who you are as a human being to the truths that lie deep within you. You are a consciousness, a soul, a transcendent self that resides in a multifaceted, multidimensional reality confederated with all matter that has existed since the beginning of time. No longer can you afford to cling to the beliefs that hold yourself in stasis. It is time in your evolution to step beyond such limited thinking and into the realm in which you really belong — a realm of limitlessness. How do you incorporate all of this into your life? How do you get to the writings of your soul and your intrinsic energetic self?

Decoding, like any other spiritual quest, does not necessarily consist of shocking events that miraculously take place overnight (although, one may certainly run across the occasional epiphany). You needn't worry about diving in and doing this deep kind of work to get the "big change." For the most part, deep soul changes are a result of commitment to the search and a gradual process that accumulates over time which produces shifts in consciousness.

As I have said, decoding the behavioral/emotional/energetic patterns that you have set forth in your life is a primary step toward creating balance and harmony. Understanding your own inner structures allows you to tap into your innate wisdom on a completely different level — a deeper, not so surface-oriented level. As your deeper resources of wisdom begin to bubble to the surface, healing and growth will begin to occur — physically, energetically, emotionally and spiritually. Even the clothing you wear can, and should, be looked at. Remember Mary Beth the client who wore the oversized red sweater with the huge black heart? We often wear that which reflects our energetic state of being. We often wear clothing that supports and matches the colors of energy that we need at that particular time. So what are you wearing today? What colors of clothes fill your closet and how do those colors coordinate with the colors of the chakras?

I often refer to the decoding process using the analogy of concrete. For instance, a relatively small piece of concrete has within its structure hundreds and hundreds of pieces of aggregate. Within the sand alone, there are billions of individual pieces affecting the whole. There is water and the concrete powder mixture as well. All of these components are parts of the whole which, when mixed together, bind to create what seems to be a hardened reality.

It is the same with your spirit, your mind, your body and your energetic system. All of them have been bound together with the pieces of aggregate from your habitualized behaviors, emotions and instinctual pressures. Decoding your inner graffiti is about taking a symbolic sledgehammer and lovingly dismantling the concretized pieces of your life so you can get to your core.

I feel that it is important for me to explain the way in which I perceive traumas that are energetically lodged within the physical body. This will allow you a potentially different perspective whereby you can work more deeply with some of the exercises. When I am in the process of intuitive/energetic assessment and looking into the chakra system, one of the many things I pick up, or see, is what I call a "rift(s)." As described in Chapter Two, the chakras are conical in shape and energetically attach to the spinal column at various locations. The conical-shaped chakra moves outward through the body and extends outside of the physical body, on average, six to eight inches. When I see a rift, it appears as if a section of the chakra's wall is out of alignment. Moreover, within each chakra there are usually a multitude of rifts. All us have them, as they are inescapable, and not necessarily bad.

Imagine, if you will, you are looking at a tree that has been cut in half. You would naturally see the rings of that tree, indicating the years of its growth. When I look at a chakra I see thousands of concentric rings which construct the body of the chakra. These rings are all stacked one on top of the other, much like those plastic expandable travel cups you can buy at the drug store. When a rift occurs within a chakra it is as if one of the rings has been jerked out of place, causing an expansion in that portion of the chakra wall, thus causing energetic swelling in that area. The swelling keeps the rift in this dislodged position and creates a holding area, a memory if you will, steeped in the emotional energy that impacted the area and forced it out in the first place. Furthermore, you create behavior to manage your situation regarding the impact of energy. Thus, what stays within the memory the chakra is the impact itself, the emotions around it as well as the behavioral components to perceptually lessen the impact.

Moreover, when you come upon an experience in which the energy currents match those of the initial emotional impact, this engages those energetically-based, emotional/behavioral components within you, bringing back the impact memory. So if something happened when you were little that had a certain emotional energetic quality, and as you grew up the same emotional energetic qualities came at you again, the rift would be reinforced. Your response to the situation — your behaviors — would be reinforced as well. By determining the location of the rift(s) as it relates to the distance from the spinal column, I can gain a better understanding of the relationship between the energy and the emotional impact, as well as the age at which the trauma took place. From this information, relationships to other chakra components are revealed and assessed, and corrective measures are applied.

A trauma can be considered to be perceptually subjective in nature. Within this context regarding a childhood issue, a trauma can be anything from falling off a bicycle and skinning your knee to child abuse. It can be an embarrassing childhood situation, or the loss of a parent. As well, it can range from a difficult childhood illness, to not getting your picture selected by your fourth grade art teacher. Moreover, what is traumatic to one person may not be perceived as such to another. Given that, you can see how it is the intensity of the emotional impact and how it is perceived (whether it is traumatic or not) that controls whether or not a rift will be created, as well as any resulting emotional/behavioral patterning. This holding of energy, packed with emotions, results in moving the energy into the physical body on a cellular level.

I call this the Energetic Emotional Impact Theory. Simply stated, this theory is based on the fact that during early stages of life, and prior to certain levels of cognitive maturation, we do not have the ability to understand what happens to us using methods of logic to pick the situation apart. What happens to us energetically is that since we didn't have these cognitive abilities to figure out what happened to us, we were left with the only thing we had — the emotions and the impact of those emotions. It is this emotional impact which affected us specifically within the chakra system.

To further explore this, you could say that when we were young, we all had certain things happen to us that were out of our control. That's the way life goes. This is one of the key components to why people have such difficulty healing early childhood issues. They simply do not have the cognitive context from which to draw upon. We can understand more easily why we were fired or why a marriage didn't work. But it is difficult to understand why we felt so abandoned as children, especially when we were told that we were loved by our parents. It is extremely difficult to figure out why we were locked away in closets, or told to go out and cut the stick from the tree so our father could whip us with it, or other horrific events. When events like this happen to a small child, most of what a person is left with are the emotions. Consequently, when work is done on those issues as an adult, emotions just pour out like thunderous floodwaters, uncontrolled and, at times, misunderstood.

To illustrate this more clearly, let's take a look at a typical childhood incident. You may have fallen off your tricycle when you were three years old. At the time, possibly your sibling(s), parents, a playmate or even a stranger may have told you that you were stupid or clumsy for falling off your tricycle. They may not have even said it in a mean way, but you may have perceived it as such. So, not only could you have scraped up your physical body, which leaves an impact, but your emotional and energetic body was injured as well by their words. That emotional impact may have really, deeply hurt your feelings; therefore, you emotionally set up the conditions for the behavioral patterning to begin its existence within a particular chakra.

As you went through your maturation process, you may have found that you were frequently getting your feelings hurt when someone would come at you with what you perceived to be hateful words — words that degraded you or your work. You may feel as an adult that you can't do something right based on someone else's opinion of your work.

Conversely, the incident may have made you more determined to try harder when you attempt new things, setting the conditions for you to become an overachiever. Any situation like this simplified one is dependent on the way in which your energy was impacted by another's energy and the way in which you perceived the event.

Situations of this type, as well as the gathering and holding of other's beliefs (which have emotional attachments), create new scripts with which you attempt to manage your life. These issues, again, are your inner graffiti, accumulating over the original writings on your soul's walls, clogging up your ability to again access your deepest soul self. Therefore, looking at the construction of the chakras and determining the locations of rifts within the system is one of the ways in which you can start the process of decoding your inner graffiti.

To facilitate your own healing though decoding your graffiti you begin the process of discerning, intuitively, your inner voices which have various tones and levels of intensity. They whisper or shout out your graffiti and are constantly vying for your attention, hoping that you will listen to them and act them out. Some of these inner voices are from your soul. Some are from the various parts of your physical body, offering you wisdom and instruction as to what to feed your body, how to move your body and the like. Some are the voices of bad habits beckoning you to eat things that really don't serve your body's health. A lot of these inner opinions are random programmed thoughts that just go on and on like a broken record playing in your head.

These repetitive voices form a meditation of sorts, and are the ones that have the most power to lead you astray from your soul's voice. That is why developing a practice of meditation is so important. You need to turn your attention inward, but not towards the lifelong meditation of the chattering mind. You need to turn toward the inner peace of the soul and the feeling of bliss as you connect deep within your heart chakra. Take time out of your day and go into this peaceful inner sanctuary. If you desire to clean up your outer world, you must take the time to tidy up what is inside of you.

A very simple yet powerful method, which will fit right into your practice of meditation, concentration and prayer, is listening to your body. Your soul's echoes will, most assuredly, speak to you through the various organs and/or components of your physical body. Listen to your body and it will tell you what you need to do for yourself. The trick is listening to and then trusting the information that is coming through. And in order to build this level of trust, you need to practice. If you do this, you will begin to hear the whispers of your soul.

It is important to keep several things in mind as you both process and progress. You need to understand that in all instances in life the power of an impact upon any system depends on the intention of the energy and the energy itself that is brought to bear. If you are examining an emotional impact that occurred during your life, you need to look at how much perceived power the energy of the situation or person had over you. In other words, how much power do you give the situation? So, in brief, there are three aspects to which you need to bring to your attention: 1) the intention of the energy coming at you, 2) the energetic impact itself and 3) your perception of the first two. That is the first set of determinations you need to make when you run across a past issue that is still troubling you today.

The inner power needed for you to grasp an understanding of your inner graffiti and to change things in your life is the power brought forth and expressed by you, backed by your will, courage and mixed with positive emotions. Granted, sometimes you need to be really brave in order to begin the process of freeing yourself. Be willing to think about being brave. As Maya Angelou said, "It takes courage to have courage." Sometimes in order to do this type of deep inner work you need to give yourself permission and the space to be where you are. So begin the process gently. You may need to simply be in a place where you are just thinking about acting on your body's wisdom or your soul's voice. That's just fine. Remember you don't have to jump into a situation with both feet. Simply be willing to look at it, and go from there. It is always a good idea to start any journey from the place in which you are currently standing.

If you have ever bumped or crashed into something, hurting your physical body, you also recognize the fact that your body is a perceived solid reality. Your current habits and the environment within your reality are perceived by you and supported by the culture as hard. However, they have been constructed and maintained by your mind and set firmly into your body. The mind then keeps you and your body bound to the illusion, which forces the perception to be maintained, occasionally retarding the healing process.

Wrap all of this around the fact that we as human beings also deal with instinctual pressures and universal archetypal forces and you have quite a ball of twine to unwind. Instinctual pressures are emotions from past lives that have not been released. They are lodged within, creating habits, feelings and fears, which can seem irrational — the fear of fire, falling, water etc. These can be trapped within and manifest themselves as either dynamic forces or frailties that percolate up and gradually find their way into our consciousness and behaviors. Behaviors such as these are blended with enculturated constructs and form the erector set of your life. Of course, these habits can be perceived by you to be either beneficial or not.

At times, you may have given up attempting to change your reality because you don't believe you can punch through its hardness. You may believe there are such severe constraints now pressing against you that you cannot be freed from them. You feel out of control and that the expressions of your mind, manifest within the body, have taken over. You feel powerless. However, you are not powerless. Your task within any reality you have built is to process and grow on a soul level within that reality. The way to move from one reality, pleasant or horrific, is to learn and embrace those soulful lessons.

No matter what you are facing you need to understand that this so-called constrained and/or habit- bound reality built up with frailty, fear and uncertainty has mental origins that are now locked in the body. But you have the key. You can unlock the door and set yourself free. You are in control of those mental origins. Yes, it most certainly can be a vicious cycle when habit-bound mental tapes replay disaster after disaster within your mind, ultimately affecting your body and environment. However, all of this negative chatter impedes your mind, enslaving you to its whims, cyclical fears and habits. You must remember that your immortal soul is in control, not your personality, your imprinting or your enculturation. You are the powerful one who has choreographed the reality in which you exist and move. You have orchestrated your lessons as this immortal soul that has been in existence since the beginning of time. You can break through seemingly hard realities.

When I was on the road to recovery from the illness that caused my NDE, the doctors told me that my eyesight would never improve. They also told me that I would probably be on medication for the rest of my life. There were lots of things they told me I couldn't do anymore. In fact some people around me suggested I apply for social security benefits because I would no longer be employable or able to work at a "regular" job. At the time of my recovery I had lost my left field of vision in both eyes. I could only see half of whatever I looked at. If I had believed the hard reality that faced me, especially when it came to the issue of my blindness, I would not be where I am today.

I was also told that I should never drive again. For me, that was all they needed to say in order for me to fight back against this hard reality. Take away my independence? Never! I decided that I would never be bound to this situation. However, the hard reality of the situation was that the external world, my doctors, the system (licensing, examinations, etc.), the way the roads are constructed, car mirrors, everything — common thought wrapped in common faith — told me I could never, ever drive again. My mind knew the reality of this new way of seeing and when I first rode in cars with someone else driving, I would miss whole lines of cars and oncoming traffic. It was a bit scary to say the least. Virtually everything in my reality, the external, my physical body, my eyes, and even my internal thoughts at the time, were working against me. I would have bought into it if it weren't for that small spark inside of me, deep inside my body and soul.

It took me four to five years to break that hard reality, but I did it and can now drive anywhere I want. They said that my eyes would never get better because of brain cell damage. Yet, they are better now. I thought them back to health. I have driven all over the country in and out of Los Angeles and Manhattan, too. I am no longer on any medication nor did I give up on being a productive wage earner for my children. My point is, please don't tell yourself that you can't do something because the external reality is too hard for you break through. You can decode it, learn your soul's lessons from it then pop that reality bubble, pushing it away. Create the quality of life you desire. You have the God-given power to do so. Believe me, I personally know about hard realities. I also know about the depth and breadth of the human spirit. You are in charge of your mind and therefore, your reality, inside and out.

Asking your body and then trusting its wisdom can bring you experiences that builds belief in your intuitive wisdom. The structure of belief that you build through these behaviors will enhance and strengthen your discipline. Often a client will be working with me and say something to the effect of his or her intuition has been telling them to eat a certain food or to do their practice or live a specific way. They ask for my opinion, which is always the same. "Commit to your intuitive wisdom and trust that." I assure them that if they need to hear their intuition speak to them on this issue a few more times that is perfectly fine. It doesn't matter if you need to hear your inner voice sing out five, fifty or six hundred more times before you act, as there are obviously lessons equal to the number of times you will hear the voice. I do share with them, as I will share now with you, that if you choose to listen more quickly you will get the bigger picture faster and move on from there without having to experience everything that could potentially be attached to the situation. But do not think there are any short cuts. You need to listen, examine and act. The processes cannot be skipped to move you along your path more swiftly. Your endeavor and commitment will move you along, allowing you to build more discipline and patience for your practice, yourself and for others.

For instance, certain food products simply do not agree with your body. Your intuition as well as your body's reaction has been telling you so, yet, your mind is saying, "Oh, just a little more," and you give into your mind. Your body and intuition will find ways to make you listen. A whispering intuitive body will, sooner or later, turn into screams of disorder or disease. Therefore, if you choose to listen sooner than later, guess what. You will have gotten the picture. You will have developed a beginning sense of discipline and you will have avoided the potentially damaging, but nonetheless, lesson-filled experiences that were possibly awaiting you.

As you begin to listen more carefully and act upon your wisdom you will realize something very important. That your body and your body's energy will always tell you the truth. It is your rather sophisticated and undisciplined mind that will take you for a ride. It is your mind that will tell you it's OK for you to have that bowl of ice cream, and then five minutes after you've consumed it will scold you incessantly for eating it in the first place. Learn to listen to your body. It won't lie to you; it simply doesn't know how to. It is like the unheard child that, at times, sits in the back of the room with its hand held steadfastly in the air, just waiting to be called upon to reveal the correct answer. The mind is the child that sits in the front, pops rubber bands at the teacher's back then smiles innocently when the teacher turns around. Trust your body's voice. Trust your intuition and then use your mind's intellectual abilities to articulate your body's intuitive wisdom toward your resolve .

9

Practices That Nurture Your Body

You are spirit housed in physical vehicle — a body...

You are already good at being a spirit...

Now is your chance to be spirit, fully engaged in a human, physical experience...

These practices are just the beginning. Like all of the methods within this book, they are suggestions for you to use to begin and/or further your process toward enlightenment. The most important task for you is to commit to your wisdom and rearrange the exercises to suit your specific needs, desires and structure(s).

I'm not going to discuss with you nutrition, herbs, physical exercise techniques etc. There is a lot of material out there on these subjects of wellness. The focus of this book is intuitive wellness and wellness through energy medicine. Combine these simple exercises with your other ideas of wellness and get ready to soar in ways you never thought possible.

Eastern practices, such as those that are found in the Science of Yoga, Hinduism, Taoism, and Buddhism say that you should protect your vital force, original energy. Be mindful of body, mind and speech. Protect and conserve vital force energy from leaking out or being misused Excessive use of chakra energy, especially creative sexual energy, through ways that are not honoring to your body, your mind or your spirit drains this energy from your body. For instance, engaging in sex for the sake of sex, or through other inappropriate agendas (trying to get someone to love them or for attention's sake, revenge on another, etc.) is unhealthy and creates bad karma as well. It will drain vital forces of energy out of the body, particularly the kidneys and the reproductive centers. This causes the body to grow weaker.

We know that the chakras control the neuro-hormonal levels of the body. When they become weaker, the body becomes weaker. As your body weakens, your willingness toward life will grow weaker as well, causing discipline, generosity, patience and mindfulness to float away from you. Nourishment on all levels will begin to wane. You are, therefore, more apt to criticize other people as judgments arise from the mind more easily, along with other negative thoughts regarding oneself.

When you become critical in this way, happiness leaves you and even more negative thoughts arise. At times these negative thoughts make you start to buy and gather excess around you. It is all a misuse of all your chakra's energy, as you become more and more attached to things, people and allow your sensory organs (seeing, hearing, tasting, feeling and smelling) rule your mind and therefore, your life.

Treat your body and your body's energy as a temple and vehicle. Treating it as a temple simply means honoring it, and not becoming a slave to it. Becoming a slave to your body, focusing on your looks or other surface issues does not bring the depth one is seeking regarding your body's innate wisdom which can lead one to a deeper sense of spiritual unfoldment. Keep your body clean. Honor your body with pure water and good food. It is a vehicle that moves your soul and pure mind around in this lifetime to achieve good deeds, merit and spiritual growth. Treat it with respect and let it work with your spiritual causes.

If your body is filled with chemicals, poor food and negative emotions which can wedge themselves within the very fibers of your muscles, your body will not perform in a manner that is in accordance with your desire to achieve enlightenment. It will break down, causing the mind and spirit to follow suit. Your treasured birth to this life is such a gift. Use your body to propel you forward toward greater levels of understanding and compassion. Treat it with kindness in speech, thought and deed. Self-respect, respect for your body/vehicle, is very important.

Love your body, in whatever form it is right now. Just as one would take a flowering plant that is undernourished and feed it, give it light and pure water to grow, you should care for your body. Rid yourself of perfection pictures regarding the way you think you should look, comparing yourself to others. Be in your body. It does you harm to try and project yourself into someone else's form or shape. That scatters your thoughts, your energy and your mind. You will never be anyone else but you. Don't try to be, or you will become filled with negative comparisons.

Be compassionate with the body you have. The more positive thoughts you place within it the more it will respond, like the plant, to your compassionate words and deeds. As a result, those actions will allow your body to take you toward a place of inner peace. You have accepted your precious birth within this body of yours for a reason. Be happy with what you have chosen to be your vehicle, lesson-filled as it may be.

Grounding Your Body's Energy — A Visualization

Just like in preparation for Running the Rainbow, it is more helpful if you feel solidly placed upon this earth. Many who are on a spiritual path love to be up in the ethers, so to speak. They love and enjoy the phenomenon of lightness and love so much that they float through their days and nights, not really touching the earth.

Long ago, when a young prince was emerged in his search for the truth of reality, he was challenged by the various faces of Maya, reality(ies) comprised of ignorance and suffering. He sat meditatively, and then touched the earth upon which he sat to show that the earth was real. As he touched the earth, Maya, illusionary reality dissolved and this young prince became enlightened. He became the Buddha.

That touch of the earth through the physical body is a goal here. After all, that is why we are in these bodies as spiritual beings in the first place. We have the notion of being spirit-like. We understand the light and the airiness of it all. What we need practice with is how to be those spiritual beings and be on the earth fully engaged and fully alive. Why else would you be here and practice this art of service to others in this way?

To ground yourself in any moment, simply visualize roots or cords moving out of your first chakras on the soles (souls) of your feet. Drop them as deeply as you want into the earth. Just let them go. After you have grounded yourself by visualizing dropping roots and cords from the soles of your feet, see, feel and know the earth's energy rising up through those grounding cords and into your body. Use the same process as you did in Running the Rainbow with respect to the flow of energy up through the body, out the top of your head, spreading through your arms and out the palms of your hands.

If you are currently suffering from a disorder or disease that is compromising your body's strength and structure, use this exercise to assist you. If you are fatigued, occasionally or chronically, use this exercise to help boost your strength and clear your body. When you are visualizing your grounding cords, drop them into or wrap them around the rocks and magma inside the earth's body. The rocks are the bones of Mother Earth. When you are hurting physically, mentally, emotionally or spiritually and you have lost your strength, connect with Mother Earth in this way — draw on her strength when yours is waning. *Always have confidence in your intuitive wisdom as it comes to you. It's your energy, it's your consciousness — trust and commit to it!*

Spinal/Chakra Breath Exercise

In my experience, this is a powerful exercise. It came to me during a time in which I was healing the remnants of a broken ankle on my right leg. It had healed reasonably well, however, I had lost a great deal of flexibility in my ankle and foot. Since I do yoga as a part of my personal practice and teach it within the context of several workshops, I was a bit discouraged to say the least. I had been to a traditional MD, and after he viewed a $1200.00 MRI his conclusion was as follows: I had lost movement in my foot and the only way to correct it was to perform surgery, which may or may not work. My inner physician was telling me that there was another way — that there was a way in which I could engage energy medicine to fix the problem. I left the doctor and went home.

The next afternoon, I laid on my healing table and told God to give me some direction. I'm still a little bossy sometimes with the universal forces. Nonetheless my request was granted. The Spinal/Chakra Breath Exercise was the result of that request.

I followed the instructions I was given through my meditation, which is given below. This was my initial experience with this exercise, its process and the result. I took three breaths of pink energy into my mouth, visualized it dropping down my spinal column into the second chakra region of my body. I held each breath for a moment or two, as well as holding the intention for complete healing. (Note: second chakra energy/consciousness is also reflected in the wrists and ankles of your body.) I exhaled my pink, energized breath out the back of my second chakra (I was doing as my body directed). While I was exhaling the third breath, my right ankle snapped, much to my surprise, and I now, and each day since, have full movement of my right foot and ankle with no pain or stiffness. Needless to say, I was amazed and grateful. I also ran to my computer to copy down the instructions for this exercise in order to share it with clients and now with you.

When I am working with an individual on these issues to correct rifts within their chakras, I use this exercise most often. While working with a client in person, I'll usually suggest the order in which to work with each chakra. However, since I am not personally with you, you will have to be the healing facilitator. Since you already are that, simply ask your body in which order you should place each chakra. Just ask, listen and trust. The perfect order will come forth for you. Simply ask your body which chakra should go first, second, third and so on, until you have placed all seven of your primary chakras.

Once you have established the order in which you will be working, there is always a setup that needs to take place as you work with each chakra. The setup is as follows:

Setup

1.   Ask whether you need to work with the front or the back of a particular chakra. (Applicable in chakras two through six only, as these are the chakras that have a front and back to their system.)

2.   Ask what color or combination of colors you need to incorporate within your breath for the purpose of this exercise. (Note: Each time you do this exercise, the colors will more than likely change. This is due to the color's molecular vibration mixing with your own breath, prana (life-force energy), and applying healing to the chakra, allowing it to change and heal. Different colors add different vibrational rates that are applicable to the variety of subtle levels of healing that are necessary for your process.)

3.   Ask how many breaths of colored energy you need to use for this particular session. (Note: the number of breaths will more than likely change each time you do this exercise.)

4.   Once you have determined the above information, proceed to the following directions.

Directions

Note the colors you have been told to use and visualize them floating in a vaporous cloud at the back of your neck (the location of both the fifth chakra and the medulla oblongata — the brain stem). Gently inhale, drawing the colored energy into the back of your throat and form it into a ball of energy which now sits at the top of the spine within the medulla oblongata. Now, while holding your breath, visualize that ball of colored energy dropping down your spinal column to the specific chakra location with which you are working. Continue to hold your breath and the intention of release and blessing. When you exhale, *see*, *feel*, *hear* or *know* the energy and breath moving from the spine, into the narrow opening of the chakra as it attaches to the spine and then out through the body of that chakra. Repeat as needed. (Since there is no spine in the head, when doing the 6th and 7th chakras simply breathe into the head, filling the entire head with colored energy. When preparing to exhale, focus the colored energy in the center of the brain and exhale out the appropriate chakra.)

To make it easier for you I would suggest that you jot down the chakra and suggested order that your body gave you and then proceed with the above-described directions.

Chakra:

Suggested order:

1.)
2.)

3.)

4.)

5.)

6.)

7.)

I strongly suggest that you write down at least your initial experience with the exercise in your journal. It will add to the depth and breadth of your information regarding the way in which energy moves through your body. Remember that you are creating an energetic map with all of these exercises. They are powerful tools which will assist you in gaining intuitive wellness.

The nice thing about this exercise is that you may not have to do a lot of cognitive processing during or afterward. This is due to the fact that this exercise deals with the energetic impact that caused a "rift" in your chakra system. Depending on the age at which the "rift" occurred, you might not have mental recollection of the incident. That is the seemingly special magic behind this exercise, which clears the energetic impact without heavy physiological processing. If something comes up that you feel you need to deal with, either by yourself or with a trained therapist, do so. It's your life — follow your body's wisdom intuitively and be well.

Eating in a Sacred Manner

Some of my students tease me because I just don't find silverware, dishes and glasses to be all that important in my life. They have come over to my home several times for class and I like to serve them food. You need fuel when you practice and play with energy and energy medicine. They think I'm strange because I only have a few glasses and I usually eat out of a wooden bowl with chopsticks when I eat at home. I either sit on a cushion at my dining room table, which sits 14 inches off the floor, or I stand and enjoy the presence of a particular tree outside of my window. I prefer eating in silence. One of the most important aspects of eating for me is to eat peacefully with no TV. If I am with guests or family, the conversation is healthy for us to eat and digest along with our food.

You need to find what feels honoring for you and eat in that sacred way as much as you can. Invite your family to discuss what would be fun and good for them. I know life is nuts and hectic at times, however, I would encourage you not to eat from a paper towel while driving down the road, over the sink (too often!) or from a clown's mouth (a drive-through window).

Your food, which of course you are now choosing intuitively at the grocery store, is there to serve you — to feed your body, mind and soul. Choose it wisely and mindfully. Prepare it mindfully. Intuitively *see, hear, feel* and *know* where your food came from: who picked it and/or processed it. Stretch your mind's eye into those places and you will discover the sacred connection that is there for you, waiting.

Create as sacred of a space as you can for you to eat in. Eat slowly, with attention and intention and you will notice a difference in the way in which you feel and the way in which your body looks. Think about all the messages your body receives if you choose to listen to the blare of commercial television, especially the news, or have unsettled family commentary at the dinner table. There is a time and a place for families to discuss issues that may end up heated, or to watch the latest bombing and worldly destruction and other sensational items. Give your sweet body a break. Don't feed it all this other stuff while you are trying to nurture it with nutrition. Not only do you need to look at what you are putting in your body, but take a good intuitive look around and see the true environment in which your have been eating in. Does it feel good to your body, mind, soul and to your intuitive self?

Be as consistent as your life's schedule allows, remembering that wherever you go, you are in a sacred space. Live from that place, eat from that place and watch your body change according to this new way of honoring it.

Standing in Nature's Power

One of the best ways to strengthen yourself is to feel the strength and power of nature. The rocks are the bones of Mother Earth. Sit, lie or climb on them and the strength of your inner and outer structure, the bones of who you are, will become stronger as well. Once while walking the ocean's shore on Whidbey Island in the state of Washington, I found a rock. It was a normal looking, gray igneous rock with white striation running through it. Nonetheless, this little guy spoke to me and fit right in the palm of my hand. At that time in my life there was more stress than I thought I could handle. You know, one of those darker periods. When I looked at this rock, and noticed its nature and structure, I realized that it, too, had some stressful times; yet, it had remained strong and beautiful. I moved forward with new awareness and strength.

As well, learn to flow with your emotions by watching the waters around you flow. It doesn't matter if you're in a crowed city. Look at the way in which the water flows out of your sink faucet and down the drain. Does it have to pass over dirty dishes all of the time, or is the water's path clear? Compare that to your life. If it is available to you, watch the rain water flow down the drainpipes of your building, through the streets, in streams, waterfalls, fountains, rivers and oceans. Water, fortunately for now and for the most part, is everywhere in some form. Watch and learn about the fluidity of your emotions through the waters of this planet, however they come to you. Learn how you flow or do not flow through your life, by understanding the structure of this natural wisdom.

I always find it interesting that when there have been what seem to be stressful releases happening, or preparing to happen within my life, my dishwashers, toilets, washing machines and sinks respond to my inner pressures and get clogged up too. Life, and the structures that bear her name, is a mirror if you dare to look.

Then there are the trees — beautiful soulful trees. Study how they rise and fall in the forest, giving birth to other trees from their rotting bodies. What a great sense of unconditional love they display. Look at their strength as they grow in the most difficult places. You too can grow within the difficult spaces of your life.

Once I was lecturing in a bookstore and someone asked me where I find God. I shared with them, with eyes filled with tears, "In the rocks and trees, in the plants and flowers and in the faces of people I see." I have always felt that my church, my sanctuary, lies in nature. One of my favorite places when I was a little girl was up in the willow tree in our backyard with my blanket and a pack of crackers. I'd sit up there, rain or shine and just be rocked by the wind and the gentle creaking of the tree.

Next time you manage to pull yourself away from the grind, which will hopefully be at least once a week, stand and breathe in the power of nature and restore yourself. I have been blessed to have lived in all of the corners of the United States and have traveled through all but four of them. There is natural beauty and magic everywhere in nature and in this country. Then of course there is the rest of the world to explore as well.

There is strength you can depend on to help heal you residing in nature. Gather it into your body. Go out there. Go intuitively to the place that calls you. You don't have to tell people you are being intuitively guided to do something unless you feel comfortable sharing that information. Just tell them you want to visit such and such a place. Go there, be inside yourself and draw from the river of life that flows through nature, cycles into you and back out again. Go with an open heart and it will be opened even further. Like most truth, the power of nature is simple. It teaches and heals.

Your Body's Optimal Wellness — A Visualization

Sit in a comfortable position, or lie down. Call all of your energy back to your body in a way that you are intuitively guided to do so, or use one of this book's exercises to help you. Be centered and get into that grounded feeling as well. Now visualize your optimal body in its most complete and well state standing in front of you, or floating above you, whichever is appropriate to your body's posture.

Now that you have that image, light up that body with the color red, the color of the first chakra. Still visualizing the optimal shape and wellness of your red energetic, chakra body, intensify the color and really make it vibrate with life-force energy. When your intuition and body's wisdom tells you to do so, allow that "red energy" body to slip into your physical body, like a hand slipping into a glove. Fully, *see, feel, hear,* and *know* the power of a well-balanced physical body, aglow and charged with red first chakra energy now inside of your physical body.

Repeat this process using all of the chakra colors. Arrange them in any order, as directed by your intuition. As well, if you are guided to do only one or a couple of the chakras, that is perfectly fine. Commit to your wisdom and trust what you are given. You can even ask your body if you need to add additional colors to a particular chakra light body, so to speak, in order for you to bring about further wellness and balance.

Like all of the exercises, play with this one when you are guided to do so. If you incorporate it into your daily life, and guide your thoughts accordingly, think of where your body will be in your future. Looking and knowing where the thoughts, intentions and attentions of your mind are directed today will allow you to discover your future.

Draining Unwanted Energy from Your Body

We all get tired and worn out at times. One of the causes of fatigue is that you are holding too much energy from other people and from the situations you have been moving through within the context of your daily life. It is wise to release that which is not yours. You will feel lighter and unencumbered.

To drain unwanted energy(ies) from your body, sit or stand with your feet hip distance apart. Initially, draw in two or three deep breaths through your nose, dropping the energy and focus of your breath all the way into the pelvic area of the body. Exhale slowly through your mouth. Now, with steady focused breath, visualize roots or cords dropping from the soles of your feet into the earth. Once groundedness has been established, visualize a third cord dropping down from your tailbone into the earth.

While staying grounded, breathing gently, yet deeply, take the focus of your attention to your seventh or crown chakra. Ask your body what color or combination of colors you need to run through your body in order to drain away all that is not yours. Listen and trust what you get. Take the color(s) and form a ball of energy slightly above your crown chakra. Allow the color(s) to then flow into the crown chakra down through the body, down your arms and out the palms of your hands (its like a reverse Running the Rainbow, with modifications). Continue with the colored energy running down through your torso and allowing it to run down your legs, out the soles of your feet and your grounding cords.

Now, the key. Once you have the energy flowing through your body in this way, know that it will continue as you move to the next focused step. Take your attention to your heart center. Ask your heart center where in your body there is any unwanted energy that is either yours or belongs to someone else. Listen and follow your body's guidance to the location(s) of this unwanted energy. If there are multiple locations that speak to you, take one at a time. You will be guided through your intuitive sense as to what locations need to be addressed and in what order you will address them.

Ask the unwanted energy if it has anything to tell you. Listen and trust. Then, when you are confident that the dialogue with this unwanted energy(ies) has run its course, bless it, bless and release anyone or thing that is attached to it and allow the unwanted energy to flow down the grounding cord that extends from your tailbone and into the earth to be changed from negative to positive.

Repeat this process as many times as you need to, for oftentimes there are several locations within the body that are storing unwanted energy. You don't need that type of congestion. It only leads to misalignments and disorders. Get it out of there. Again, as you go from location to location, be aware that colors may change. Your liver area may need red to run through your body, while your lower back may need a combination of green and blue. Trust your body's wisdom, adjust as you are guided to do so and clean yourself out.

All of the exercises in this book are designed to be easy to use. As I always tell students and clients, once you get the mechanics down, I encourage you to do each exercise whenever you are called to through your body's wisdom. You and your body, spirit and mind want wellness. Wellness requires maintenance because your internal and external environment is constantly changing, as all things do. All things are impermanent. Please make this and other exercises in wellness a part of your daily life.

The Power of Movement

I am not here to tell you how you should move your body. I'm just going to share with you that you need to MOVE IT. Daily! Whatever calls to you, do it. Whether it is Yoga (and there are many flavors of Yoga being taught today), Tai Chi, Qi Gong, biking, rowing, weights, jogging, dance or whatever, just please move your physical temple around the block a few times. The energy within the chakras and nadis will move as you move your body. The congestion within the organs and within the alimentary canal (which runs from the mouth to the anus) will begin to cleanse and become healthier. From there, your blood will not be so filled with toxins that have seeped back in from an unhealthy small intestinal tract or colon. Honor your body and move it. Don't wait until your body shakes you up by screaming at you through a disorder or disease. Ask your body what exercise process it would like to engage in and do it.

While you are out there moving your body, breathe. Breathe deeply, dropping the energy of your breath into the pelvic area of your body. Restore and vitalize your body by breathing in this way. Inhaling deeply through the nostrils, *feeling, seeing* and *knowing* you are dropping the energy of your breath to your body's pelvic floor and then exhale through the mouth sending the air out of your body with a quick strong "HA." More energy and thought forms can be released when you inhale and exhale with the intention of releasing negativity and then breathe through the body in this manner.

Perhaps you can think of it this way. Primarily, when you are moving your body you are engaging the consciousness levels of the lower three chakras, as they govern the physical. When you incorporate consciousness and deep breathing in this way, energetically bouncing your breath down to your first chakra, you will clear the negatively perceived thought forms that are getting stirred up as you move your body. As well, you will be reinforcing the positively perceived ones.

For instance, if you are currently weighing a little more than you want and/or your body is not in its best form, when you starting moving your body (through a planned exercise program or more ordinary movements) pay attention to the thoughts that come streaming through your mind. Are they the kind that tell you how out of shape your are, insulting you?

Know that as you hear them they are offering you an opportunity to release them. Breathe them away. Breathe down into the first chakra, (you have to get through the upper ones to get there, so it affects them as well) and hold the intention of releasing all negative thoughts that have held you back in the past. Use the power of your breath, your mind, the will of your spirit (which holds your internal doctrines of truth) and the movement of your body to release the negativity from your body in this way.

When you work on a body level to release things you will move your life, dramatically. After all, we are in a physical world and need to deal with it. If you ignore your physical body it will come back at you, sooner or later. In third dimensional reality the body wins, because it is your soul's mouthpiece. It wins as we will all give our flesh and bones back to the soils of the earth at some point in time. It wins, of course, until you reach a higher state of consciousness, but by then you are so in harmony with your body and environment there is no separation between your body, your mind and your spirit, so hard third dimensional reality is not a problem. You live and die consciously. Nonetheless, in the meantime move your body, breathe your issues away and awaken your consciousness.

Energetic Protection Techniques

Let me talk to you a bit regarding protection techniques. Those of you who have been on a spirit-led path for a while probably know about the bubble technique. For those of you who don't, one of the more common energetic protection techniques is to place a bubble of light (any color of light but white light is used more often) around your physical body. You can make this bubble of light around you as large or as tight fitting around the physical body as you like. I would also suggest that if you use this technique you allow the base of the bubble to go underneath your feet enough to really cover you from head to toe, in a cocoon-like manner.

This is a particular technique is certainly viable and I encourage you to use it no matter where you are on your path of evolution. I would, however, encourage you to develop a strong practice that nurtures your soul, mind and body. As you continue on, progressing and moving beyond the phenomenological approach to your path, your inner core of energy will be so connected and so strong that the protection you seek will naturally emanate from the inside out. Nonetheless, use the bubble protection technique as a tool in situations that you feel warrant it, or when you need a little extra boost to ward off the external stimuli that are always pounding your energetic field. It is always good to seek a little more protection when you know you are stepping into a situation where you understand that your energy may be compromised.

If you have a busy household with lots of people running in and out all of the time, or if you have an office frequented by clients or coworkers, the following technique should be helpful for you. You can protect your environment by placing bowls of salt water around your home or office.

That salt will act as a magnet, absorbing negatively charged energy. When you intuitively know it's time to change the water, simply do so, wash the bowl, refill with more salt and water and return it to its place within your environment. Salt, like the ocean's waters, is charged with negative ions, which give the atmosphere/environment a positive feeling. Think about how healing it is to be in or near the ocean, or how the air feels after a thunderstorm. Those elements fill and charge the atmosphere with negative ions. Even though it sounds counterintuitive, negative ions are a good thing.

Moreover, if you have discordant conversations or negative thoughts around your office or home, you will feel them. What you are then feeling (again, this sounds counterintuitive) are positive ions in your environment. Salt water will assist you in changing this. It is subtle, but it is the subtle charges of negative energy that build up over time that cause misalignment in the first place.

When I work with diseases that are heavily charged energetically and/or very prevalent within someone's body, I often wash my hands with salt water after working on them. Salt, of course, is alkaline in nature. Disease is acidic. If you are currently doing energetic healing work and contacting disorders that are related to the immune system and other biochemical imbalances it is a good idea to wash up with salt water. Sea salt is my first choice, regular table salt, Epsom salts and baking soda follow.

If you have had a particularly rough day, whether you do healing work or not, take a sea salt bath. Mix some herbs and fragrant oils into the water and relax. If you are a shower person, or don't have too much time to soak in a tub, pour some sea salt into the palm of your hand and rub the sea salt over your body. Always pay particular attention to the chakras, front and back, as well as any specific areas to which your intuitive wisdom guides you.

In addition, you can wear white sage on your body to protect you. Slip it into a shirt pocket, into your bra, or pants pocket. You can even create little sage sacks to make wearing sage a little less messy. Simply take natural cloth and cut it into 4x4 inch squares, and place a small amount of sage in each cloth square. You can either roll them up and tie them with a piece of string, or sew the edges closed. You can pop these sage sacks into your dresser drawers to protect your personal items, or place them in strategic places throughout your living space. Placing them in corners, closets or places in your living space that you feel collect energy are excellent places to place these sage sacks.

Many people burn white sage or desert sage for protection and for clearing the energy fields around their body or within their living space. Fill a sea shell or a flame-retardant bowl with the sage, lighting the herb just enough to start a small flame, then extinguish the flame and allow the smoke from the sage to fill the air in the room or rooms that you are clearing. Needless to say, you need to be very mindful when you are working with fire around yourself or your home. Burning sage does a wonderful job and it feels so good to lightly fan the sage smoke through your energy field as well, clearing and purifying your energetic system.

In addition, a wonderful combination of herbs to clear an environment is: sage — for clearing; lavender — for beauty; cedar tips — for blessing; and sweet grass — for protection. Simply combine the four herbs together, light the herbs briefly, let the flame extinguish and allow the smoke to fill your living space. Furthermore, when you are using sage by itself, or a combination of herbs to smoke out the negative energies in your living space, make sure you not only act responsibly around the fire, but you may want to open your windows or doors to allow both the air and negative energy to move through and out of the space.

I have had instances in the past when I have been clearing space and did not have sufficient movement of air. Because of that lack of openness, doors and windows rattled, slammed and banged around (with no external, windy weather), which of course scared me to death at first. So always check for the flow of air and energy within a space before you begin clearing it. Negative energy has to have a place to go when you are bringing in a more loving and God-centered energy. Make room for it and open a window or door a little bit to allow the forces you don't want in your space a more peaceful exit.

When you are doing any clearing and protection of your energetic space either around your body or your living space, always say prayers, blessings and words of gratitude. Call in your God force energy, your angels or other divine force(s) that please and resonate with you. It is your space. Create a wonderful one energetically. You'll notice the difference.

Listening To and Understanding Your Body's Point of View

This is an exercise that will help you tune into the voices and wisdom that are within your body — your body's organs, bones and muscular structure. By being able to listen in to the conversations that are going on within your body, you will be better able to understand and therefore, make clearer choices as to what your body may need in order to bring about your wellness. This exercise, like all of the exercises in this book, is intuitively driven. It will allow you open intuitively even more so, in order to become clear. You will be able to use this exercise when attempting to resolve issues within the many areas of your life. You may wish to approach such areas as what foods you need, who or what supports you and your environment, as well as in what directions should you place your energy, attention and intention.

To work with this simple exercise, simply find an area of your body — a particular chakra, organ or region of your body — that has been speaking to you. Remember that your body will probably be speaking to you through one or more of the following mechanisms — physical pain, discomfort or disease. Once you have found the place within your body that you will be conversing with, take a few deep breaths into that area of your body. Then ask the highest level of consciousness within that area what it is trying to relay to you. Ask any question you have.

Ask from the perspective of your spirit and body, i.e. "Spirit (or Body) of the first chakra, what do you want or need for me to do in order to rebuild my life?" Or "OK stomach, what is it you are trying to tell me? Why do you hurt?" I know it sounds a little strange, but just flow with it. There are a lot of answers inside of us if we would just take the time to ask direct questions. Some of your answers may seem arbitrary and you may not understand what you body is trying to tell you, at least not right away. After all, you two may not have been on speaking terms for a while. We are all in such habits of pushing our bodies around, even though there are the subtle whispers and groans from it which encourage us to slow down, eat something besides junk food, and get out into nature more.

I highly suggest that you do not, at least for the initial stages, ask what the mind wants. It has been directing your life with its wishes that have most assuredly been created from the graffiti within you. Your mind is unruly at times; it will take you all over the place if you have not taken the time in mediation to understand your own mind's patterns and processes. So ask your spirit and ask your body what they need. They are the two components of the triune of self that have been the least heard. They are the parts of you that will never lie to you.

After you have had a few moments of conversation with your body, or body part, write down the answers you get and start reprogramming your mind based on the information your body and spirit have given you. Look this over carefully and then create a plan that will allow you to take action on the intuitive wisdom you have received. Create affirmations and positive thoughts regarding this information. These things will assist you in moving into a more positive direction by realizing that the answers you seek are within you and you can create your wellness — intuitively, of course.

10

Creating Intuitive Wellness

Everyday you get the chance to trust yourself more...

Wrapped within this chapter are concepts offered for your daily contemplation which will assist you in creating, supporting and maintaining your intuitive wellness. To draw it all together for you, remember that intuitive wellness is the art of creating wellness within all areas of your life, based on the knowledge you derive from your internally guided, cosmically connected and God-realized well of wisdom. Go into the silence of yourself daily and ask for the intuitively guided wisdom you need to create and support your wellness in that day. Mindfully take it one day at a time, no matter where you perceive your wellness to be.

We are only here for a short while. A lifetime seemingly goes by slowly when you count the minutes and hours. However, the months and years whisk by and you wonder where it has all gone. Enjoy and embrace it as compassionately and robustly as you possibly can. It can all change, swiftly. We will all go to the place in which we are hours away from death, then taste the empty sweetness of holy light pouring from a place which lies beyond physicality. Nothing is permanent. If you have lived even for just a short while, you know that life can be full of tornadic activity, literally and figuratively. All can be lost within moments. One should, therefore, live in the moment, embracing it with all the wisdom one has, then share that wisdom with others.

There is a wonderful old movie called "Auntie Mame" wherein exists one of my favorite sayings: "Life is a banquet and most poor suckers are starving to death." Life is so rich and full of multidimensional experiences and reminds us, through such experiences, to let go of our perceived harder realities, our egocentrism, and embrace the love of God more fully. I urge you to let go of the things to which you find yourself so attached. If they are meant to be in your life, and this can be things or people, they will not leave you. People, objects and situations, like the threads of fabric, weave through our lives. The very nature of the weaving and interaction will hold or not. You can mend and patch, but if the tear is meant to be, it will happen. So be at peace with the way in which objects and people move through your life.

I am not, however, speaking of renunciation of your life. You do not have to give away all that you have accumulated. Realize, however, that that to which you are so heavily attached will leave you at some point in time. When there is heavy attachment, there will be suffering when it leaves you. That is a natural process of the mind. You can, through the use of your mind and intuition, ease the suffering by finding that your mind is the impetus of your thoughts which can spin into thoughts of attachment and suffering. You can, therefore, use that same mind as your pathway to peace by changing your thoughts.

As you practice detachment, joy, freedom, balance and an unburdened perspective about life and who you are will emerge. Use your innate wisdom and allow the synchronicities of life to flow through you and not be pushed so far away by your rational mind. They will lead you to where you are supposed to be and accordingly, your life will be fuller. Furthermore, if you are attached to doing things a certain way or having certain things and people around, you may not hear the voice inside of you calling you down another path to service and peace. Listen deeply, intuitively and daily to your truths. Do not pass by life's banquet table, filled with the delicious expressions of God.

Enlightenment is achieved by working in a disciplined manner on your spirit-led path. This is not necessarily an easy task, especially within the context of Western culture. One of the reasons that your daily spiritual practice, in whatever form it takes on for you, is so important is that it is your connection to what is more true about your life than the articles and objects you may have spent years collecting and placing around you. The truth which comes from the innate wisdom that lies deep within you, mirroring the cosmic mind, is your centering device that will assist you in maintaining balance within your being

In order to find wisdom and wellness, close your eyes, and with your intuitive mind, read from the book of your soul — your internal doctrines of truth. The truth and answers you seek will come forth in boundless waves. Seek the wisdom from the thought forms that reside within the atomic structure of your being, which is sometimes coagulated as matter. No matter if you are peering into the atomic structure of your energy or your body, they will be, nonetheless, filled with thoughts.

Truth and wisdom reside within the atomic particle of thought. It cannot be joined with or assimilated by your denser senses of the body or intelligence unless those senses — smelling, seeing, hearing, tasting, feeling — are joined first with your intuition. There is, of course, wisdom in the sensations of the body and mind, but to reach the depth that is God-realized, your search needs to be intuitively guided into the infinitesimal parts of yourself and your atomic and subatomic light/energy reality. In order to accomplish this journey and obtain that which you desire, you need to practice daily.

For daily intuitive wellness, I suggest you incorporate whatever exercises from this book that speak to you, or anything else along your path that echoes your truths. Set aside anywhere from twenty minutes to an hour one to two times per day and do your practice. Again, these particular exercises were created with application in mind. They are designed for you to use daily, from moment to moment as you are internally directed to so. They will bring your intuitive development to a more heightened state, allowing you to attain deeper levels of awareness, attentiveness, mindfulness, etc.

You will get to the place that reflects your intention, as your intention will always manifest and demonstrate itself within your physical reality. Therefore, if you want to succeed with the development of your intuition for your daily wellness and abundance, you will need to place both your intention and your practice in a more prioritized place within your daily schedule. If you want to be a better basketball player, you practice. The same is true for the development of your intuition. You practice. I understand that as most of us work through very busy days, it is easy to push your inner work to the side, leaving it there to collect dust. However, the dust that is collecting is really inside of you, shutting you off from your desires for happiness and creating suffering.

Open yourself to amazing possibilities. These exercises are so adaptable to other postures besides sitting in a quiet room, undisturbed. Get creative with them and your time. The goal is to be centered, mindful and gaining in enlightenment all the time, not just when you are in a quiet room or in a more formalized sanctuary or church. In my view, the church, sanctuary and monastery are inside of you. Therefore, you take them with you within every context in which you find yourself.

The Spiritual Teacher

Life and the experiences held within each moment are your teachers. Again, you can learn a lot about unconditional love by looking at the way in which a tree has fallen to the forest floor, creating a nursery out of its body, so to speak, for the new trees. You can discover more about kindness towards your body by watching animals. All animals gently stretch and check in with their body and their surroundings before bounding off to start their day, chasing after their catch.

People float in and out of our lives all the time, for moments or years, teaching us, as you and I are teachers to one another. We have sacred contracts born from and directed by karma and soul-level agreements to meet and assist in one another's growth. We have all had those instances when we have met someone and we could swear we had either met them before, or had known them for years. These types of relationships are comfortable for us, like an old pair of slippers or a worn pair of jeans. They take form, slipping right into one another's presence and heart, for however long.

We have many types of teachers in Western culture, yet, within our culture's non-secular institutions some people find themselves feeling empty and unfulfilled from the teachings. It is vitally important to have a spiritual path as we collectively move forward together. That path, naturally, may or may not be a traditional religious path. It really doesn't matter what path you take. If you just ask, your spirit will guide you. Your spirit has to feel well on your chosen path in order for you to feel well physically, mentally and emotionally. It has to feel right to you, deep down inside. If it doesn't, commit to the wisdom surging inside of you and start searching for more answers.

As you are searching, it is important to have a sense of what a spiritual teacher should feel, look and be like for you. For instance, the desire of a true spiritual teacher is that of guiding you towards your own awakening. As you begin to awaken to your own innate wisdom, obtaining enlightenment, divisions between you and your teacher will diminish. You will become as one. All of the masters report this. Christ shared this view. Lord Buddha speaks of it as well. The role of the teacher is to show the students, who loves, believes in and is dedicated to finding within the wisdom of God, that they can achieve all they desire by endeavoring and being disciplined on their path toward oneness. The teacher demonstrates self-realized oneness with God and directs, with their essence, the students toward experiences from which they will grow. As the students devote time and effort, they too will be able to do deeds as great, or more so, than the teacher. Entire philosophies are based on this and other supportive precepts.

You are not to be engulfed by your teacher or by his or her personality. If you are feeling consumed, talk to your body, mind and spirit and commit to your own wisdom, making sure that your wisdom is not steeped in or tainted by a hurt ego. In short, be honest with yourself regarding the situation. A good teacher will demand that you pull your own spiritual weight, yet embrace and support you as you move forward. By looking deep within yourself for answers, you will merge from your soul's darkest night with your own true nature, which is the nature of God. Again, as this process comes forth, any perceived polarities that had divided you from your teacher, as well as those lines that create divisions between ignorance and enlightenment, will soften and wane.

Make no mistake about it, it may not be easy as spiritual teachers assist you in stretching your consciousness — which may or may not be perceived as something that feels good to you in the moment. Nonetheless, they will stretch you with love, because they can see the level(s) of consciousness that you are here to work on as well as able to obtain. They desire nothing more for you than to achieve peace and enlightenment for yourself and for your soul.

It is up to you to choose your spiritual teachers wisely. Be certain that you are ready to commit to your wisdom as well as to commit to learn from your teachers' wisdom. Know that like other things or people in your life, you may not need to be under your chosen teachers' wings for a long period of time. For instance, I worked with five other people and a teacher for one hour a week for eight weeks with the intention to develop my clairvoyance more. For me, it didn't take long to get settled with all that I had been doing and seeing in the years prior to that time. It may or may not be that way for you. Perhaps, it may be years before you feel you are ready to fly on your own. That is why it is so important to develop your own sense of intuition, so you are clear inside about what teacher you should work with and for how long.

A good teacher will let you go and soar, even if you crash. If you don't crash, at least any more than normal, the teacher will be pleased for you. They know that you are not theirs, and that you have your own mission and destiny to live out. This is only one lifetime, in-between other lifetimes. Your highest and most holy obligation is to your soul's enlightenment and then to the souls of others. Do as much as you can to evolve yourself toward oneness and share what you have learned in a kind and gentle way with whomever wants to listen and share the experience with you.

A spiritual teacher should be like a mother/father and will demonstrate honest caring for you. Do not confuse childlike attachments or codependent feelings with those feelings of honor and trust for your teacher's wisdom. Remember that you are seeking guidance from someone with whom you resonate. If there is no resonance, do not go there and engage. Find another teacher and always intuitively query the teacher within, your wisdom, as to the direction you should go.

Some people give up on a teacher and think they now know it all and can go on. In some cases that is true; the teacher has served the student for that particular lesson or series of lessons and it is time to move on. However, in other cases it is the student's ego grabbing them around the neck. If there is conceit, envy or disrespect lurking in the heart and mind of the student, then it is time to look deeper into the ego.

If that has happened to you, look honestly at yourself and the situation. It is healthy to have ego in the sense that you have a balanced sense of self. It is the selfish ego, the demanding childlike ego that I am referring to here. Look at what is within the teacher or situation that reflects and brings up those emotions within you. Have you seen or felt them within other contexts of your life? Look at it. Be with it. Grow from it. More than likely, your teacher is assisting you in your own clearing.

There should only be love inside of you as you move toward God and enlightenment. The other stuff has to get out of the way and out of your body. When you feel boundless love and joy inside of yourself for your teachers you know you are clear with them and there is no karma. At that point in time you can move on or stay, whichever you like. When you love your teachers with that much joy, they will always be in your life, at some level. Always love and honor your teachers, whether you have been in their presence for five minutes or fifty years. They have taught you something and that should be acknowledged and honored. A good teacher will certainly honor and acknowledge the teachings they have received from being in your presence and well as the teachings they have received from their teachers.

Never give your power away to a spiritual teacher. Give love, respect, compassion and honor. That is what your teacher should give to you, always. A good teacher will empower you and assist you in realizing your God-given wisdom and strength. Then he or she will encourage you to share what you have learned with others, in your own way, using your own essence.

A teacher may not give you everything you ask for in regard to process or technique when you ask for it. Sometimes teachers will know exactly where you are and what you need. You need to decide whether or not you can be with that. Never forget, however, that you are your own best teacher and healer. If you have dedication to God, in whatever form that is for you, and to your path, you will find your way through the muck and mire. If you choose to work with physical teachers, know that they will assist you in dealing with the path, but they won't necessarily make your path easier.

Know that your greatest teachers will be the discoveries which lead to what innately lies inside of you. Be thankful for the blessing of being alive and know that with the power of your mind and truth of heart you can change your world and help others do the same.

But by all means, seek out a spiritual teacher if you are called to do so. A teacher should demonstrate that which you wish to become — and understand that that which you seek is already within you. It is within you, or you would not have seen it in your teacher. Ask the Universe to send you a formal teacher if you want one and don't already have one. Be very clear on your intention when you ask, but ask if that is your desire. One or more will appear in your life, as if by magic.

When your teacher arrives, in whatever form, remember you asked for the teacher and teachings. Pay homage and be grateful. Participate as fully as you can, using your innate wisdom and your facilities of reason to discern both the teacher and the teachings. In Buddhism, the sutras (which are Buddha's teachings orally given to his disciples then ultimately put into written form) remind us to do the following:

- Do not rely on the individual teachers, rely on the teachings.
- Do not rely on the words, rely on the meanings.
- Do not rely on the adapted or conventional meaning,
- Do not rely on the ultimate, absolute meaning.
- Do not rely on intellectual knowledge, rely on wisdom.

Follow your innate wisdom and grow from the experience of having a spiritual teacher.

Knowing Your Truths

By now it is crystal clear that in order to discern all that you need and want to do in order to be intuitively well, you have to know what inner truths assist you on your path. Here is a simple exercise I would like you to try. It has been helpful for me and has seemed to assist others as they reevaluate their footsteps of truths along their pathway.

What follows is a list of personal truths. This is a list of my truths, reflections of my teacher within. I suggest that you, too, make a list of your truths. My list is taped to my desk and when I am not flowing as well as I would like to through my day, I'll look at them. The truths I'm not following so closely will light up for me. It allows me to take pause and realign myself, allowing a sense of inner peace to be reestablished.

If you are not following your truths, you may not feel as well as you could. Again, you basically know what you want out of your life, and therefore, you should understand what the underlying truths are those things which supports you on your journey. It is imperative to know them, see them daily and embrace them always. Here are my inner teacher's truths.

Commit to my wisdom and trust it

Live in the moment, mindfully

Honor myself, daily

Listen to the birds

Watch the clouds

Remember the bigger picture(s) of life as I move through daily situations

Remember my purpose and my work

Endeavor to bring peace within and without

Remember and be who I am

Sing

Feel compassion for all beings

Go into the silence of myself, daily

Listen

Jump for joy

Know that abusive situations wear many masks, love my way through them

Stand up for my rights, feelings and purpose

Share with others

Balance money and things

Live simply

Give service

Have fun
Hug trees
Be in awe of the sky and land around me
Honor animals without hips and shoulders
Keep moving my body, daily
Eat in a sacred way
Keep in contact with those I love
Be honest, with myself and others
Live happily
Sadness is a clue, listen
Honor my emotions as well as my mind
Write
Obtain and share knowledge
Listen to my guidance
Discern
Honor ceremony
Set a sacred space for myself, always
Honor the paradox in life
Move beyond phenomena
See through maya (illusion)
Be free
Share love
Keep on
Dig deep
Reach high
Think unlimited thoughts in directions that move me
Go for it
Spread joy

Eat from wooden things
Stay humble, but not quiet
Roar
Weep
Stay on my path, but know that forks exist
All paths lead to the same door, there are just different knocks
Glow
Get into the energy of life
Practice attentiveness of the mind, always
Be generous

You must make an effort within your daily practice and life to be happy, releasing negative thoughts as they arise in your mind. Practice virtuous actions of generosity, patience, moral discipline and endeavoring, concentrate in meditation and trust in your innate wisdom — your intuition. As you become a more seasoned practitioner you will not be affected by external pressure and your emotions. Therefore, you will become free. Free to assist others on their path without judgment or criticism. Even if they are childlike in the sense that they have not realized, as of yet, their personal causes of suffering. You will be filled with compassion and will be able to guide them along. Your life will exemplify more happiness to others as you remain peaceful inside, as you stop hate and anger from taking over your thoughts.

Whenever a negative or unsettling thought arises, move your focus more into your practice (a practice you never leave in the first place). Bring forth from your mind an antidote for your anger or unsettledness. Some such antidotes are the exercises and practices contained in this book. Any and all feelings of compassion and joy are, as well, antidotes. Wash your mind with compassion and know that the negative feelings will hold no strength over you.

Be willing to share knowledge with others. Furthermore, know that when others offer you advice, whether you take it or not, they are demonstrating that they are your teacher. Make note of their acts of kindness and sharing. Be a disciple in all that you do and with whom you come in contact with. You never know who is a Buddha or angel in disguise. Do not behave this way out of fear, but out of the knowing that all souls, all minds, are connected as one and have been so since beginningless time. This person with whom you are engaged has most likely crossed your path in prior lifetimes. Show them the respect their soul deserves and they will learn from you as well. Let go of your ego and sense all of the happiness there is to be found while appreciating someone else's achievements.

You have, over the course of many lifetimes and life experiences, created the karma and the wisdom you currently have within you. This dictates the levels of consciousness you are able to perceive and achieve. With that being said, stretch your consciousness as far as you can, then endeavor for more. Work through the struggles and attached phenomena associated with any particular level of consciousness. Each time you arrest the negative emotions that arise in your mind, replacing them with thoughts and positive action, actions that are of benefit to others, you gain more of the pure cosmic mind — the mind of God.

You have a circle of people that you will touch during this lifetime. You are their guardian, as they are yours. Love them. Respect them and hold them deeply with your heart. The experience of near-death and the joining with other's souls, along with other experiences in my life have demonstrated over and over again to me that we don't die. Our souls live on and on, growing and evolving. The more we can consciously tap into our soul-level existence, the more virtuous actions can be brought forth. The desires to have and to hold objects or people in our reality fade as awareness of emptiness and impermanence, along with the knowledge of our eternal souls, comes forth more effortlessly. This is all gained through spiritual practice. Even if these words resonate truth, to whatever degree, do not puff up your chest too much with pride. Even if you have learned what seems like a lot so far, there is so much to learn and so little we really know. Stay humble in your endeavoring. Everyone and everything is your teacher, respect that. Grow from that. Above all, be kind, generous to others and to yourself.

Your eternal, heartfelt soul flows like a river throughout eternity. It is like a stream, which when left unrestrained will follow its own natural impulses, drifting and rushing toward the ocean of wisdom — the one true source. Do not confine your stream of heartfelt consciousness with negative thoughts or emotions. If you restrict this part of yourself, you will become stagnant, putrid and slowly kill off all life within you.

When you are in that condition, who would want to drink from your waters of knowledge and experience? Who would want to drink and nourish their life from your tainted and thickened reservoir? Open your heart, love and be loved, which will allow your soul, mind and body to flow towards wellness, enlightenment and peace.

Life can be very simple...
The body can be brought to wellness by
drinking clear water,
moving your muscles and bones regularly
and by eating pure foods.

The mind can be brought to wellness
by the usage of correct speech, internally and externally,
as well as the attainment of peace
brought forth through learning the art of the detachment.

The soul can be brought to wellness
by endeavoring, discipline
and a daily spiritual practice.

About the Author

Laura Alden Kamm is the founder of Intuitive Therapeutics™, an intuitively-based healing system. Laypersons and physicians from across the US and abroad. request her skills as a medical intuitive, healer and educator. Ms. Kamm lives in Scottsdale, Arizona. You may contact her at 480-367-8264 or via email at founder@energymedicine.org. Her web page is www.energymedicine.org.